OKANAGAN COLLEGE LIBRARY

03624871

D0555339

THE KHRUSHCHEV ERA, 1953–1964

OKANAGAN COLLEGE
LIBRARY
BRITISH COLUMBIA

The Khrushchev Era
1953–1964

MARTIN McCAULEY

LONGMAN
LONDON AND NEW YORK

Longman Group Limited,
Longman House, Burnt Mill,
Harlow, Essex CM20 2JE, England
and Associated Companies throughout the world.

Published in the United States of America
by Longman Publishing, New York.

©Longman Group Limited 1995

All rights reserved; no part of this publication may be
reproduced, stored in a retrieval system, or transmitted
in any form or by any means, electronic, mechanical,
photocopying, recording, or otherwise without either the
prior written permission of the Publishers or a licence
permitting restricted copying in the United Kingdom issued
by the Copyright Licensing Agency Ltd.,
90 Tottenham Court Road, London W1P 9HE.

First published 1995

ISBN 0 582 27776 0

British Library Cataloguing in Publication Data

A catalogue record for this book is available from
the British Library .

Library of Congress Cataloging-in-Publication Data

McCauley, Martin.
    The Khrushchev era : 1953–1964 / Martin McCauley.
      p. cm. -- (Seminar studies in history)
    Includes bibliographical references and index.
    ISBN 0-582-27776-0
    1. Khrushchev, Nikita Sergeevich, 1894–1971. 2. Heads of state-
-Soviet Union--Biography. 3. Soviet Union--Politics and
government--1953–1985. I. Title. II. Series.
DK275.K5M28 1995
947.085'2'092--dc20
    [B]   95-10405
                                        CIP

Set by 7 in 10/12 Sabon Roman

Produced through Longman Malaysia, GPS.

CONTENTS

EDITORIAL FOREWORD

Such is the pace of historical enquiry in the modern world that there is an ever-widening gap between the specialist article or monograph, incorporating the results of current research, and general surveys, which inevitably become out of date. *Seminar Studies in History* are designed to bridge this gap. The books are written by experts in their field who are not only familiar with the latest research but have often contributed to it. They are frequently revised, in order to take account of new information and interpretations. They provide a selection of documents to illustrate major themes and provoke discussion, and also a guide to further reading. Their aim is to clarify complex issues without over-simplifying them, and to stimulate readers into deepening their knowledge and understanding of major themes and topics.

ROGER LOCKYER

NOTE ON REFERENCING SYSTEM

Readers should note that numbers in square brackets [5] refer them to the corresponding entry in the Bibliography at the end of the book (specific page numbers are given in italics). A number in square brackets preceded by *Doc.* [*Doc.* 5] refers readers to the corresponding item in the Documents section which follows the main text. Words which are defined in the Glossary are asterisked on their first occurrence in the book.

LIST OF MAPS

ACKNOWLEDGEMENTS

The publishers would like to thank the following for permission to reproduce copyright material: Little, Brown and Company and Andre Deutsch Ltd for five extracts from *Khrushchev Remembers* by Nikita Krushchev, copyright © 1970 by Little, Brown and Company; Little Brown and Company for several extracts from *Khrushchev Remembers: the Glasnost Tapes* by Nikita Khrushchev, copyright © 1990 by Little, Brown and Company, translation copyright © 1990 by Jerrold L. Schecter; the School of Slavonic and East European Studies for an extract from *Khrushchev and Khrushchevism* by Martin McCauley, copyright © 1987; and R.A. Medvedev and Blackwell Publishers for an extract from *Khrushchev*, copyright © 1983 by R.A. Medvedev.

While every effort has been made to trace the owners of copyright material, in a few cases this has proved to be problematic and so we take this opportunity to offer our apologies to any copyright holders whose rights we may have unwittingly infringed.

PREFACE

The demise of the Soviet Union in 1991 highlighted the failure of President Gorbachev's efforts to reform the Soviet system. He had attempted very bold and daring reforms of the Party, industry and cultural policy but had only succeeded in unravelling the whole edifice of Soviet power. His predecessor, Yury Andropov, had attempted some mild reforms, but one has to go further back to Khrushchev to find another Soviet leader who was as daring and bold as Gorbachev. The main driving force behind the Soviet bureaucratic system, Stalin, had left a flawed legacy in 1953. Reform was inevitable. But what shape should it take? Beria was the first to perceive that de-Stalinisation was necessary. He was cut short, but this may have been a loss to the country. Khrushchev won the battle for primacy in the Party and state and launched his initiatives. He did battle with the ministries which were dominant. He tried to make the Communist Party more accountable and bureaucrats in general more responsive to the needs and aspirations of the population. However, he only changed aspects of the system, not the system itself. His lack of trust in the market meant that his economic reforms tried to do something very difficult, if not impossible – namely, make the planning system much more effective. He decentralised because he had faith in the creative abilities of managers, workers and peasants. He had a dream, communism. His Utopianism led to his proclaiming the dawn of communism in 1980, mainly to beat the Chinese to the gates of paradise. In foreign policy he practised peaceful coexistence but threatened the Americans with his non-existent missile fleet. His debunking of Stalin critically weakened the regimes in eastern Europe and made it very difficult to reform. He fell out with the Chinese, who became his bitter critics. The communist movement became polycentric. His cultural policy blew hot and cold. His conservative critics had a point when they warned Khrushchev that his reforms, especially the ending of the infallibility of the Communist Party at the Twentieth Party Congress, risked setting in motion the destruction of Soviet power. All of them could be swept away in the flood. He was an original thinker and addressed many of the fundamental problems of the country. However, his impact was limited. If there is such a thing as a brilliant failure, he was a brilliant failure.

NOTE ON RUSSIAN NAMES

Russian names consist of a first name, a patronymic (father's name) and a surname. Hence Nikita Sergeevich Khrushchev or Nikita, the son of Sergei Khrushchev. A sister would have been called Anna Sergeevna (the daughter of Sergei) Khrushcheva. Khrushchev's wife was Nina Petrovna, Nina, the daughter of Petr (Peter), née Kukharchuk. (Kukharchuk is a Ukrainian name, hence does not end in the feminine 'a'.) Another Russian name is Rimashevsky (masculine) and Rimashevskaya (feminine). The latter denotes both the daughter and the wife.

Many Russian names end in 'ov' and 'ev'. This is the genitive plural. Khrushchev, pronounced Hru-schoff, has an 'ev' ending because it follows 'shch' (one letter in Russian). The stress is at the end, on the 'ev'. He would have been addressed formally as Nikita Sergeevich, as the title *gospodin* (mister or lord) had been dropped in 1917. It is now again in use in Russia. He could also be addressed as Tovarishch (Comrade) Khrushchev.

Most Russian names have a diminutive. Sasha for Aleksandr, Misha for Mikhail, Nadya for Nadezhda, Tanya for Tatyana, and so on. Children, animals and close friends are addressed with the diminutive. There is also Ivan Ivanovich Ivanov: Ivan (John), the son of Ivan Johnson. Donald MacDonald, Donald, the son of Donald, would be Donald Donaldovich Donaldov in Russian.

Ukrainian names sometimes end in 'a' (e.g., Kuchma) but this is both masculine and feminine. Kukharchuk is masculine and feminine. Some names end in 'o', e.g., Chernenko (Chernenkov in Russian). There are also names ending in 'enko', 'chenko', 'lenko', denoting the diminutive, e.g., Kirilenko, little Kiril or Cyril; Mikhailichenko, little Mikhail or Michael. A common Armenian surname ending is 'yan', e.g., Mikoyan; the stress is always at the end. Common Georgian surname endings are 'vili', 'adze', 'elli', e.g., Dzhugashvili (or Djugashvili); Shevardnadze; Tseretelli. Muslim surnames adopt the Russian ending 'ov' or 'ev', e.g., Aliev, Kunaev, Rakhmanov.

THE COMMUNIST PARTY AND THE GOVERNMENT

There was always tension between the Communist Party and the Soviet government over which was the dominant institution in the state. Lenin, as chairman of the Council of People's Commissars (Sovnarkom), perceived the government's function to be that of running the country. The Communist Party was responsible for ideology and supervision of the government. The primacy of government continued during the 1920s, but when Stalin won the struggle to succeed Lenin he reduced its autonomy. This also happened to the Communist Party. The government's task was to implement the policies of the Stalinist leadership. However, in May 1941, Stalin decided to become chairman of Sovnarkom (Prime Minister), and he remained so until his death in March 1953 (in 1946 Sovnarkom was renamed the USSR Council of Ministers). Malenkov then became Prime Minister and head of the Party. He was obliged to divest himself of one of these offices and he chose to remain Prime Minister, thus identifying government as the dominant institution. His main opponent was Khrushchev, whose power base was the Party. When Khrushchev won this struggle it was inevitable that he would choose to strengthen the Party at the expense of the government, thereby reversing the roles of these two institutions. A major reason for this *démarche* was to make government accountable to him and the Party. However, he quickly discovered that real economic power in the Soviet Union rested with the ministries and that economic reform could only be effective if the ministries agreed – in other words, if it did not challenge their power and privilege. Khrushchev became Prime Minister himself in 1958. In 1964 it was agreed that the same person could not be head of the Party and Prime Minister simultaneously. This was observed until the demise of the USSR in 1991. The Party was acknowledged as the dominant institution. However, it lost its economic functions in 1988, and its power and influence were further undermined in 1989 with the election of the USSR Congress of People's Deputies (parliament) and the elevation of Gorbachev to the executive presidency in 1990. The Party was in utter disarray from 1989 until its banning by President Yeltsin in the aftermath of the failed *coup* of August 1991. The power of the USSR ministries on the territory of the Russian Federation passed to the Russian ministries.

The USSR was sometimes described as a Party-government state. The main features of the relationship between the Party and the government are shown below. The approximate equivalence of Party and governmental bodies is given at each territorial level.

Party	Government
Presidium (Politburo between 1966–91), Communist Party of the Soviet Union	Presidium of the USSR Council of Ministers
Central Committee (CC)	USSR Council of Ministers
CPSU Congress	Presidium of the USSR Supreme Soviet USSR Supreme Soviet
Republican (e.g., Ukrainian) Party Secretariat	Republican Council of Ministers
Republican CC	Presidium of Republican Supreme Soviet
Republican Party Congress	Republican Supreme Soviet
Regional (*krai* or *oblast*) Party Committee	City, *krai* or *oblast* soviet
Regional Party Conference	
District (*raion*, etc.) Party bodies	*Raion*-village soviet
District Party Conference	
Primary Party Organisations (enterprises, collective farm, etc.)	No governmental equivalent
Rank-and-file Party members	Voters

For Marta

PART ONE: THE BACKGROUND

1 FROM PEASANT BOY TO A MEMBER OF STALIN'S ELITE

Nikita Sergeevich Khrushchev was born into a peasant family on 17 April 1894, in the village of Kalinovka, in Kursk guberniya. As with many other growing families, the smallholding was not large enough to support them, and his father, Sergei, was obliged to spend more and more time away from home looking for work during the winter. Like any other peasant boy Nikita Sergeevich became acquainted with work at an early age.

> Whenever I see shepherds tending their sheep now, my own childhood comes back to me. I remember looking after sheep too. ... The shepherd used to send me out, saying: 'Right, Nikita, run and bring the sheep in' – and that is just what I did. ... I used to look after calves too. (*Pravda* 19 May 1962)

In 1909 his father decided to become a coal miner in a pit in the Donbass region of Ukraine. This brought Khrushchev's rural life and his formal education to an end. The family moved into a small, single-storey house outside Yuzhovka (named after the Welsh entrepreneur John Hughes, renamed Stalino in 1924 and Donetsk in 1961. During Khrushchev's visit to Britain in 1956 he was struck by the rows of red brick houses, just like those he had seen in his youth, except that all but the windows were covered in ivy.) The town, with about 40,000 inhabitants, was growing rapidly as an industrial centre and becoming a magnet for peasants seeking a better life. Life was dirty and hard, but prospects were good. Nikita Sergeevich had to take any work that was going, and at the age of 15 he became an apprentice fitter at the Bosse factory, which was owned by Germans. He was to help repair mining machinery from the local pits.

Khrushchev's political education began early, in primary school. His teacher, Lidiya Shchevchenko, was an atheist who undermined his strict Orthodox upbringing. The Communist Manifesto, by

Marx and Engels, not surprisingly greatly impressed him when he borrowed it from a fellow worker in Yuzhovka. Memories of the failed 1905 Revolution were still alive in the town and the Bolsheviks began to be active. In 1912 Khrushchev was a strike leader in the Bosse company, but it failed and he was sacked. He could not find factory work and was obliged to turn to the mines, working as a fitter in the French-owned Rutchenkovo pit. Most politically active miners in the mine were pro-Bolshevik. Khrushchev's drive led to him becoming a miners' leader and a major strike was called in the Rutchenkovo mine in March 1915. The miners won, but this made Khrushchev a marked man. He became a regular reader of *Pravda*, the Bolshevik Party newspaper.

Although many miners were called up when war broke out in 1914, Nikita Sergeevich was not. Increasing labour shortages led to prisoners-of-war, especially Czechs and Austrians, being sent down the mines. He became acquainted with the concept of Pan-Slavism, that all Slavs are brothers and should not be fighting one another. Among Slavs, the Czechs had the highest opinion of the Russians. This faith was to be cruelly shattered only in 1968 [*Doc. 6ii*].

The revolution of February 1917 was greeted with unbridled joy. Khrushchev was elected to a soviet* of workers' deputies at Rutchenkovo and quickly became a leading light. Although he was not yet a Party member, he supported the Bolsheviks. In December 1917, Khrushchev became chairman of the Union of Metal Workers in the mining industry. With the onset of the civil war in the summer of 1918 he became leader of the Rutchenkovo miners' battalion and also joined the Bolshevik Party. He was soon appointed a political commissar and played an active role in the bloody civil war in the south. It was a formative experience for him and he always had a special affinity for military men.

When he returned to Yuzhovka and the Donbass after the civil war he found a devastated region. To this wider tragedy was added a personal one. His wife, Evrosinya (they had married in 1914), died of typhus in 1921, leaving him a son and a daughter to bring up on his own.

ACQUIRING QUALIFICATIONS

Khrushchev quickly realised that his lack of technical qualifications would limit his advancement and he managed to get the Party to send him to the Yuzhovka Workers' Faculty when it was set up. However, he was not going as a mere student. He was elected Party secretary and political leader of the institute. He was not destined to make things. He was destined to organise people so that they could make things. His family life also entered a new phase. He married Nina Petrovna Kukharchuk, a lecturer at the Workers' Faculty. They were to have three children – a son, Sergei, and two daughters, Rada and Elena.

The first engineers graduated from the institute in 1924 but, although Khrushchev was a member of the award-making body, he did not receive a diploma. His aptitude for Party work took precedence and in 1925 he became first secretary of Petrovsko-Mariinsk *raion**. This ensured his inclusion in the Ukrainian delegation to the Fourteenth Party Congress in Moscow in 1925, a great occasion for Nikita Sergeevich. It was his first visit to the capital but there were no luxuries. Delegates slept on planks, stacked together like logs. The secretary of the Kharkov delegation slept with his wife in a row like the rest and this led to some ribald remarks. Khrushchev showed he was the country bumpkin on his first day. He got on a tram to the Kremlin and ended up nowhere near it. After that he decided to walk, even though it could mean missing breakfast. The Ukrainian delegation was headed by Lazar Kaganovich and their paths were to cross and criss-cross often during the next forty years.

The Congress was notable for a violent struggle between Stalin and Zinoviev, head of the Leningrad delegation. Khrushchev supported the 'General Line', in other words Stalin, and helped to howl down the secretary general's opponents. Stalin made a great impression on Khrushchev and he was especially struck by Stalin's apparent modesty and fair-mindedness. Khrushchev was also a delegate to the Fifteenth Party Congress in 1927, which saw a fierce struggle between Stalin, Rykov and Bukharin – the right – and Zinoviev, Kamenev and Trotsky – the left. The Ukrainian delegation was solidly on Stalin's side and the delegation was briefed – behind closed doors with all non-Ukrainian communists excluded – about the present stage of the struggle and the tactics to be adopted at the Congress. Rykov, to underline his support for Stalin, hit on a gimmick. He presented the secretary general with a steel broom: 'I hereby hand this broom to comrade Stalin to sweep away all our enemies.' Little was he to know that Stalin would sweep him away a decade later. Zinoviev and his supporters were defeated and many expelled from the Party.

In early 1928 the Ukrainian Party leadership, then in Kharkov, was on the lookout for good proletarian elements to counterbalance the influx of officials from intelligentsia backgrounds. Khrushchev was therefore appointed deputy head of the organisation department, responsible for cadres*. However, he did not take easily to the work:

> It was nothing but paperwork. I'm a man of the earth, a man of action, a miner. I'm used to working with metals and chemicals. I have a constitutional block against clerical work – it's completely alien to me. I hate having to go through a pile of forms and files to see the flesh and blood world [57 *p. 27*].

He kept on asking for a move and the following year he moved to Kiev, again as deputy head of the organisation department. It was his first visit to Kiev, and on arrival he rushed to the banks of the Dnieper, suitcase still in hand, to gaze at the famous river. Kiev was a difficult posting as it was a hotbed of Ukrainian nationalism and there were great economic problems. Nevertheless, Khrushchev deployed his increasing interpersonal skills to good effect. If his career was to take off he would have to get to Moscow, the capital of the communist universe. When he heard of the founding of the Industrial Academy, there was no holding him. The launch of the first Five Year Plan in 1928 meant that communists with technical qualifications would be in the driving seat for promotion. He pestered the Ukrainian Party leadership until it gave in and recommended him for a place.

KHRUSHCHEV IN MOSCOW

The Party organisation in the Academy was dominated by the 'Right deviationists', headed by Bukharin. Khrushchev was committed totally to Stalin, and this led to the Academy trying to give him the push. It was suggested that he was unqualified since the goal was to train senior management. Perhaps he could move to Marxism-Leninism in the Central Committee* institute. He would probably have been turfed out but for the support he received from Lazar Kaganovich, who was now a secretary of the Central Committee and a very tough Stalinist indeed. 'All Stalin had to do was to scratch Kaganovich behind the ears to send him snarling at the Party' [57 *p. 41*].

Khrushchev soon became secretary of the Party organisation, and lost no time in transforming the Academy into a battleground for Stalin's 'General Line'. Resolutions passed at Party meetings often appeared in *Pravda* the next day, and this brought Khrushchev's name to the attention of the Moscow Party organisation and the Party Central Committee. He enthusiastically supported rapid industrialisation, forced collectivisation, the sentencing of the Industrial Party, accused of being hired by the French, and the guilty verdicts passed on 'bourgeois specialists', accused of retarding the industrialisation drive. A fellow student at the Academy was Nadezhda Alliluyeva (mother of Svetlana Alliluyeva), Stalin's wife. Amazingly, few knew that the attractive, modest woman who travelled to classes by tram was the wife of the secretary general. Nikita Sergeevich and she got on very well and she undoubtedly talked about him to Iosef Vissarionovich.

Khrushchev had friends in high places – (Kaganovich had become Moscow city and *oblast** (gorkom* and obkom*) Party leader) – and also his performance at the Academy led to his election as first Party secretary of Bauman *raion* (raikom*) in 1931. His academic career had only lasted fourteen months, but it is fair to assume that he spent little time there on theoretical studies – he later claimed that his life was so busy that he had no time to read books. Instead he gained valuable political experience and graduated with first-class honours in Stalinism.

Khrushchev only stayed six months in Bauman *raion* and was then elected first Party secretary in the famous Krasnaya Presnya *raion*. He took over from M. N. Ryutin, who had put together a vitriolic attack on Stalin and Stalinism, known as the Ryutin Platform. Nikita Sergeevich extinguished all remnants of Ryutinism in the *raion* and made it safe for the Stalinists. In January 1932 he became second secretary of Moscow gorkom. He was elected to the Central Committee at the Seventeenth Party Congress in 1934. He was now a member of the Party élite. Promotion soon followed. He became first Party secretary of Moscow gorkom and second secretary of Moscow obkom. As such he was now Kaganovich's deputy. This state of affairs did not last long as Kaganovich soon departed to take over a crisis sector, Soviet transport. It was almost natural that Nikita Sergeevich should succeed him and become the master of Moscow city and the surrounding *oblast*.

Why was Khrushchev so stunningly successful? There is some truth in what Nikita Sergeevich referred to as his lucky lottery ticket. Had the Academy been in Stalinist hands he might never have entered its portals. Had Kaganovich's career not prospered neither would his, since without a patron he would not have progressed. Had the factional battle been lost he would have found himself down a pit again. He discovered that it is better to be a 100 per-cent politician – either for or against. Never dilly dally: 'I was a hundred per cent faithful to Stalin as our leader and our guide. I believed that everything that Stalin said in the name of the Party was inspired by genius, and that I had only to apply it to my life' [*57 p. 25*]. However, he would not have climbed the Moscow ladder if he had merely sung odes to Stalin. He delivered. The Moscow press wrote of his great dynamism and persistence, his 'Bolshevik toughness' (a euphemism for ruthlessness towards friend and foe) and his ability to impose discipline and inspire sacrifice from subordinates and the Moscow population at large.

KHRUSHCHEV AND STALIN

Khrushchev became a frequent visitor to Stalin's home after becoming Party leader in Bauman *raion*. These were not mere social occasions, as wives and girlfriends were not invited. Nadezhda Alliluyeva's suicide in November 1932 was a terrible shock to Stalin and the others. Stalin had a caustic tongue and delighted in abusing Lenin's widow, Krupskaya, and Lenin's sister, both of whom had supported Bukharin. He informed Krupskaya that the Party was contemplating appointing someone else as Lenin's widow! Nikita Sergeevich had to develop great skill in judging how and when to bring a subject up with the master. Stalin never engaged in a general debate about policies. He identified certain problems and invited comments. He ensured that no one was privy to all these discussions. Life was very hierarchical. When Khrushchev became Moscow Party boss he was addressed as Com. Khrushchev in a Moscow newspaper. He was an 'outstanding representative of the post-October generation of Party workers, educated by Stalin'. The article continued: 'Under the guidance of that notable master of the Stalin method of working, Comrade Kaganovich, N. S. Khrushchev has grown step by step with our party in recent years and is a worthy leader of our glorious Moscow Party organisation' (*Rabochaya Moskva*, 9 March 1935). Khrushchev is first mentioned as Com., not Comrade. That was reserved for Kaganovich. The highest plaudits of all were for Stalin: Comrade and initials are superfluous in his case. The hierarchy is here clearly spelled out. Khrushchev is not yet in Kaganovich's league and no one is in Stalin's league.

  Nikita Sergeevich was now in one of the key Party posts but he was continually under the gaze of Stalin. The *vozhd** or boss took a particular interest in architecture and engineering. After a May Day parade it was brought to his attention that many foreign guests had been greatly discommoded by the lack of conveniences. He immediately ordered Khrushchev to build forty urinals in the city (ladies were expected to make other arrangements). Moscow was a huge building site during the 1930s and one of the great achievements was the building of the Moscow metro. Begun in 1931, it was running in the mid-1930s and was a marvel of contemporary engineering. It was to serve three functions: a transport system; an underground palace to provide a foretaste of the communist tomorrow; and an air-raid shelter should the capital be bombed. It also provided a great psychological boost to the building of socialism. However, its construction exacted a fearful price as safety precautions were thrown to the winds in the race to meet targets. Thousands of workers were killed and injured. Khrushchev was in the thick of the construction process and led by example.

At the Seventeenth Party Congress in 1934 Stalin lost his title of secretary general and reverted to secretary. Some delegates approached Sergei Kirov, the popular Leningrad Party leader, to stand for Party leader, but he turned it down and informed Stalin. He was murdered on 1 December 1934, and the People's Commissariat of Internal Affairs (NKVD)*, now firmly in Stalin's grip, was let loose in Leningrad. Five hundred Leningraders confessed to the murder and a quarter of the population was arrested. The broom was applied to Moscow and the old nobility and middle classes were booted out of town, beginning in 1935. Khrushchev was in overall charge. This was mild compared to the mayhem of 1937 and 1938 when millions were killed or arrested – including 62,000 Party activists in Moscow. All the arrest and death warrants had been signed by Khrushchev, who knew some of the victims personally, but his language was as vituperative as that of Kaganovich or Molotov. 'These despicable traitors infested the Party apparatus, and some of them were actually members ... of the Moscow Party committee' (*Rabochaya Moskva*, 8 June 1937). It was part of Khrushchev's task to tramp around the gaols, accompanied by the NKVD. He encountered many former colleagues there. One, Treivas, was an 'intelligent, capable, decent man' but he did not 'escape the mincer when the butchery began in 1937' [*57 p. 69*]. The Show Trials were the greatest show in town during the late 1930s. The Old Bolsheviks, the generation who had made the revolution, were wiped out, as Stalin feared they might make a comeback should things go wrong.

Why did Khrushchev, one of the elite, not do anything to stem the tide? Was it due to moral cowardice, political myopia or a desire to preserve his own hide? Did he actually believe that it was all for the good of the cause? Part of the answer is to be found in the Khrushchev–Stalin relationship. It was one of master and servant – or, as Khrushchev graphically put it, it was one of boss and errand boy. Stalin mesmerised the unsophisticated Moscow Party leader: 'I was literally spellbound by Stalin. ... Everything that I saw and heard when I was with him bewitched me. I was absolutely bowled over by his charm' [81 *p. 18*]. This does not exonerate Khrushchev of complicity in Stalin's crimes. He failed the Party and the country, and only came to realise this in the 1950s. However, Khrushchev was always walking a tightrope with Stalin, who was notoriously suspicious, indeed paranoid. Khrushchev himself was once fingered by Nikolai Ezhov, head of the secret police.

> I was standing around and Stalin came over and asked, What's your name? Comrade Stalin, I said in surprise, I'm Khrushchev. No, you're not, said Stalin, brusquely. Someone tells me that you're really called so-and-so. I can't remember the Polish name he mentioned, but it was completely new to me. How can you say that Comrade Stalin? I replied. My mother is still alive. You can ask her. You can check at the plant where I worked, or in my village of Kalinovka, in Kursk. Well, he answered, I'm just telling you what I heard from Ezhov [60 *p. 38*].

This took place at a time when Polish communists were being liquidated as class enemies.

FORGING LIAISONS

In order to be politically effective and to gather intelligence on the way the wind was blowing Khrushchev had to develop the skills of coalition-building. Coalitions are like concentric circles. The inside one is the tightest, with succeeding ones becoming looser. The inner coalition included Nikolai Bulganin, chairman (mayor) of the Moscow soviet executive committee between 1931 and 1937 and then prime minister of the Russian Federation, whose capital is Moscow. Another important contact was Georgy Malenkov, a Moscow obkom official between 1930 and 1934 and then deputy head of the Leading Party Organs of the Central Committee. Something else bound them all together. Their patron was Kaganovich.

The 1936 Soviet constitution, the most democratic constitution in the world according to Stalin, transformed local government. Previously soviets had the twin function of making and implementing policy. Now policy was to be made at the top and local soviets were to implement it. At the first meeting of the USSR Supreme Soviet*, in January 1938, Khrushchev was elected to its Presidium*, underlining the fusion of Party and state functions under Stalin. Concurrently a Central Committee plenum (signifying that all members were invited to attend) met, and at this much more important meeting Nikita Sergeevich was elected a candidate member of the Politburo*. This meant that he could speak at sessions but could not vote. This was, however, rather academic since Stalin was not in the custom of calling for a vote in the Politburo. Although January 1938 was the date of Khrushchev's formal election, he appears to have been attending Politburo meetings since 1935.

BACK TO UKRAINE

Promotion went hand in hand with a new assignment. Khrushchev was appointed acting Party leader in Ukraine in January 1938 and his task was simple: bring Ukraine under Stalin's heel. There had been great resistance to collectivisation and the terrible famine of 1932–33, deliberately promoted by Moscow, had cost more than 8 million lives. The purges wreaked havoc in Ukraine. For instance, the Party leadership had been eliminated by the end of 1937. In June Khrushchev was confirmed in office and appointed first secretary of Kiev obkom. Only three of the previous year's eighty-six members had survived. Khrushchev made it very clear what his priorities were: 'I pledge to spare no effort in seizing and annihilating all agents of fascism, Trotskyites, Bukharinites, and all despicable bourgeois nationalists in Ukraine.' He was clearly very successful, since the Party newspaper reported that the 'merciless uprooting of the enemies of the people – the Trotskyites, Bukharinites, bourgeois nationalists, and all other spying fish – began only after the Central Committee of the All-Union Communist Party sent the unswerving Bolshevik and Stalinist, Nikita Sergeevich Khrushchev, to lead the Central Committee of the Communist Party of Ukraine' (*Sovetskaya Ukraina*, 12 March 1938). Heady stuff, but the conclusion is inevitable: Khrushchev was wallowing in blood.

The year 1939 brought war, and the Stalin–Hitler Pact led to the

Soviet invasion of Poland and the acquisition of western Ukraine, almost all of which had formerly been part of the Russian Empire. Khrushchev became a political commissar, charged with purging the region and packing off many Jews, Poles and Ukrainians to Siberia and Central Asia. Industry and trade were nationalised and agriculture collectivised. In June 1940 Romania disgorged Bessarabia and northern Bukovina. The Ukrainian-populated parts were added to Ukraine and the rest became the Moldavian Soviet Socialist Republic. Khrushchev was much more perceptive than his master about the likelihood of war. Stalin persisted in the belief that Hitler would keep his word, and ignored warnings about the imminence of a German attack.

WAR

The German invasion of 22 June 1941 transformed Khrushchev into a political-military commander. He became the Kiev Military District commander's no. 2 and as such had the right to participate in all key military decisions. Each military unit had a political commissar and he was subordinate to Khrushchev. War meant that the military became Khrushchev's main concern. The Party, government, industry and agriculture remained his responsibility, but its focus changed. The primary goal was to organise for victory. The military took its orders from the General Staff, which in turn, took theirs from Stalin as commander-in-chief. Khrushchev was a vital link in the military chain and had access to the *vozhd* both as a political commissar and as Party leader of Ukraine. An essential task was to move as much industrial capacity, transport, equipment and so on as possible to the Urals, Siberia and Central Asia. About one-third of industry in the soon-to-be-occupied areas was transferred east. Khrushchev played his part in this extraordinary feat.

It took Stalin about two years to learn modern mechanised warfare. In the early phase of the war he made some egregious mistakes. Khrushchev did his best on the Ukrainian front but lost several battles with Stalin. For example, the military and he wanted to abandon Kiev to the advancing Germans and then regroup elsewhere, but the *vozhd* would not hear of it. This led to heavy losses. On another occasion Khrushchev wanted to call off the Kharkov offensive in March 1942, after German forces had threatened to cut off advancing Red Army troops. He telephoned Stalin twice but could get no higher than Malenkov. According to Khrushchev, Stalin refused to come to the telephone. The advance continued and led to a serious defeat, with the loss of more than 150,000 prisoners. Khrushchev was ordered to Moscow and feared the worst. The storm passed, however, and he was appointed to the Stalingrad Military Council and sent off to organise defences. His main task was to boost morale, and he displayed great courage in traversing the front under fire. After the epic victory at Stalingrad, a turning point in the war, Khrushchev moved to the Southern Front and played his part in several successful offensives and the liberation of parts of Ukraine. Lieutenant-General Khrushchev was awarded his first military decoration, the Order of Suvorov, second class, for 'skilful and courageous execution of military operations' [81 *p. 37*]. Victory at Kursk, the greatest tank battle the world until then had seen, permitted the Red Army to go on to the offensive until the end of the war. It opened up the road to Kiev, which was liberated on 5–6 November 1943. Khrushchev entered the burning, shattered city with the troops and immediately began the task of reconstruction. The Red Army carried on advancing but Nikita Sergeevich's war was over. In 1944 he became chairman of the Council of People's Commissars of Ukraine, or Prime Minister, while retaining his position as first secretary of the Communist Party of Ukraine. He was now master in Ukraine, but he in turn was subordinate to the master in Moscow.

REBUILDING UKRAINE

The Ukraine Khrushchev returned to was in an appalling state. After using it as a theatre of operations for three years, the Germans had attempted to destroy everything of value when retreating. Many Ukrainians had welcomed the invading German army, but Berlin failed to capitalise on resentment against Moscow and quickly alienated the population by its brutality. However, a Ukrainian Insurgent Army was formed in western Ukraine, annexed by the Soviet Union in 1939, and it continued armed resistance against Soviet forces until the early 1950s. The region was also the stronghold of the Ukrainian Catholic Church which vigorously opposed fusion with the Russian Orthodox Church. The nationalists exacted a heavy toll and the Soviet authorities lost 19,000 men. When the nationalists captured a Red Army soldier they were wont to boil him in water. Khrushchev outdid the opposition in brutality and became known as the butcher of Ukraine. Resistance was only crushed after hundreds of thousands of Ukrainians were deported to the east. One of the lessons drawn by Khrushchev from his experiences during the war was that the excesses of the 1930s had been misguided. Properly led, the common people were capable of great deeds and sacrifice, but they needed to feel that they were participating in something beneficial to them. This was to lead to Stalin branding Khrushchev a populist.

Agriculture was afforded high priority in the bread basket of the Soviet Union. Khrushchev quickly became an agricultural expert and fell in love with maize, trying to promote it everywhere. This led to his being disparagingly referred to as a maize freak. The weather unfortunately was not on Nikita Sergeevich's side. The drought of 1946 halved the grain crop and there was widespread hunger, even some famine. (This was kept from the outside world as Stalin did not wish to reveal that the Soviet Union was in difficulty.) Khrushchev appealed to Stalin for help, but to no avail. Stalin always bore Ukraine a grudge. It had resisted collectivisation, many had welcomed the Germans and nationalism was endemic. Rumours were put in circulation in Moscow that Khrushchev was becoming a Ukrainian nationalist.

It never rains but it pours. This proverb proved true for Khrushchev in 1947. The most serious setback to his political career occurred in March 1947 when he was dropped from three of his posts: first secretary of the Communist Party of Ukraine, of Kiev *oblast*, and of Kiev city. However, he remained Ukrainian Prime Minister. No accusations were made in public about Khrushchev's shortcomings: it was simply stated that he was being relieved of his Party posts. It looked as if Nikita Sergeevich was being prepared as the sacrificial lamb for Ukraine's failures. The person who replaced him turned out to be Lazar Kaganovich. Khrushchev was seriously ill during the summer, and this gave Kaganovich free rein. However, the unexpected again happened. In December, Nikita Sergeevich was reinstated as Party first secretary but not in his Kiev posts. A new prime minister took over. It is unclear why Khrushchev managed to weather the storm but it is another example of his remarkable talent for escaping from tight situations under Stalin. In his memoirs Nikita Sergeevich is tellingly malicious and vindictive about Kaganovich. The latter always protected his own backside while putting the boot in elsewhere [Doc. 1]. Kaganovich was very skilled at flattery and a good judge of Stalin's moods.

Kaganovich used to throw back his chair, bring himself up to his full height and bellow: Comrades, it's time to tell the people the truth. Everyone in the Party keeps talking about Lenin and

Leninism. We've got to be honest with ourselves. Lenin died in 1924. How many years did he work in the Party? What was accomplished under him? Compare it with what has been accomplished under Stalin! The time has come to replace the slogan: Long live Leninism! with the slogan: Long live Stalinism! While he would rant on like this, we would all keep absolutely silent and lower our eyes. Stalin was always the first and only one to dispute with Kaganovich. What are you talking about? he would say, How dare you say that! But you could tell from the tone in Stalin's voice that he was hoping someone would contradict him. ... Stalin liked to rebuke Kaganovich with the following comparison. What is Lenin? Lenin is a tall tower! And what is Stalin? Stalin is a little finger! Sometimes when he made this remark he substituted an analogy which, shall we say, isn't suitable for recording here [57 p. 42].

KHRUSHCHEV AND ANTI-SEMITISM

Stalin was known for his anti-Semitism but so also was Khrushchev. The latter kept silent about the massacre of Ukrainian Jews by the Nazis at Babi Yar and was responsible for the deportation of many Jews from Ukraine in the late 1940s. Khrushchev paid such scant attention to the living conditions of surviving Ukrainian Jews that they had become intolerable by the spring of 1944. It was left to Beria to instruct him to remedy the situation.

BACK IN MOSCOW

In December 1949 Stalin brought Khrushchev to the capital as first secretary of Moscow obkom and made him a Central Committee secretary. The *vozhd* may have been concerned to clip the wings of Georgy Malenkov and Lavrenty Beria, both of whom had benefited from the death of Andrei Zhdanov in August 1948. Stalin had launched the Leningrad affair (the wide-ranging purge of the Leningrad apparatus and of Zhdanov's supporters in Moscow and elsewhere), partly on their advice. They provided incriminating evidence against the victims which Khrushchev later declared to have been fabricated. Stalin may also have brought Khrushchev to Moscow because he was alarmed at Khrushchev's success and popularity in Ukraine.

Stalin engendered friction between Khrushchev and Malenkov by giving the former the rural brief. Malenkov was technically Party secretary for agriculture but had little practical experience of the rural sector. Nikita Sergeevich launched a bold initiative by ordering the amalgamation of small kolkhozes (collective farms) into larger ones. This would promote efficiency through economies of scale and would narrow the gulf between town and countryside, as investment would serve a wider area. The number of kolkhozes in Moscow *oblast* declined from about 250,000 to 100,000 by 1953. (Another explanation for this policy may be that the leadership was becoming alarmed at the continued emphasis by peasants on the boundaries of their former holdings before collectivisation. Amalgamating kolkhozes would help to eradicate memories of these former holdings.) Khrushchev wrote an article in *Pravda* in 1951 in which he discussed construction problems facing farms and appeared to be promoting the construction of *agrogoroda* or agro-towns. The following day *Pravda* published a note stating that, 'due to an editorial oversight', it should have been made clear that 'Comrade N. S. Khrushchev's article' was for 'discussion only'. Since every reader of *Pravda* was aware that editorial oversights do not occur, it signified that Stalin personally had intervened. This possibly occurred after someone, most likely Malenkov, had convinced the *vozhd* that Khrushchev's proposals threatened his authority.

Stalin's intervention could have had lethal consequences for Nikita Sergeevich, but again he weathered the storm. He records that one of the *vozhd*'s methods of judging whether someone was guilty was to make a serious accusation and look straight into the person's eyes. He was searching for any sign of guilt [Doc. 2]. However, Nikita Sergeevich did not cringe when he was accused. On the contrary, he went on the offensive. This obviously stood him in good stead on many occasions.

At the Nineteenth Party Congress in October 1952, the first since 1939, Khrushchev reported on changes in the Party rules. These included changing the Party's name to the Communist Party of the Soviet Union. Malenkov delivered the main report since Stalin was not capable of standing long at the rostrum. He grasped the opportunity of sticking his knife in Khrushchev by again criticising the agro-town project. Stalin proposed, in Malenkov's report, the appointment of a large Presidium. This omitted Molotov and Mikoyan, but it did include Khrushchev. There was to be an inner group of five – Stalin, Malenkov, Beria, Malenkov and Khrushchev – to solve the country's most pressing problems. This fuelled speculation that the boss was manoeuvring to decapitate the old leadership. All those not in the inner circle were in danger.

(In his 'Secret Speech' at the Twentieth Party Congress [*Doc. 11*] in 1956 Khrushchev accused Stalin of beginning preparations for a wholesale purge [*63 p. 78*]). A 'vigilance campaign' was launched after the Congress [*Doc. 3*]. The 'Doctors' Plot', in January 1953, accused mainly Jewish doctors of murdering Andrei Zhdanov and plotting to kill others, including, of course, the *vozhd* himself. (It was later revealed that it had been fabricated by the Minister of State Security, probably aimed primarily against Beria.) Khrushchev carefully monitored public reaction to the 'plot', and Party archives reveal that a wave of virulent anti-Semitism had taken hold of the country, with demands being voiced that Jews should be removed from their posts and shot. Party officials added fuel to this fire by calling for vigilance. This was probably promoted by Khrushchev himself.

THE END OF STALIN

Stalin had a great fear of death. When one of his doctors examined him in early 1952 and suggested that he take a rest he became furious. His suspiciousness and paranoia increased as he aged. One of the doctors who took part in the post-mortem concluded that he had been suffering from a severe hardening of the arteries for some time.

> I suggest that Stalin's cruelty and suspiciousness, his fear of enemies, loss of ability to assess people and events, and his extreme obstinacy were all the result to some extent of the arteriosclerosis of the cerebral arteries. ... An essentially sick man had been running the state [*65 p. 172*].

On 27 February 1953 Stalin attended, without his retinue, a performance of *Swan Lake* at the Bolshoi. The following evening he watched a film in the Kremlin with Beria, Malenkov, Khrushchev and Bulganin, after which they all repaired to Stalin's dacha* at Kuntsevo for supper. Khrushchev describes what happened next:

> Supper lasted a long time. Stalin referred to it as dinner. We finished about 5 or 6 a.m. – it was usual for those dinners to end at that time. ... We said goodbye to Comrade Stalin and departed. I remember that when we were in the entrance hall Stalin came out as usual to see us off. He was in jocular mood and joked a lot. He waved his index finger or his fist and prodded

me in the stomach, calling me Mikola. He always used the Ukrainian form of my name when he was in good spirits. Well, we left in good spirits too, since nothing had happened during the dinner. Those dinners did not always end on a happy note [56 *pp.* *131–2*].

The next day was a Sunday and Khrushchev stayed at home expecting a call. That evening he was awakened by a call from Malenkov informing him that Stalin's guards thought that something was wrong. Khrushchev drove to the dacha and met his colleagues there. They were told that the guards had found Stalin on the floor and had lifted him and placed him on a sofa. Khrushchev implies that they all believed that Stalin was drunk, as was his wont. Then they all went home. Later Malenkov phoned again stating that the guards were worried that something was seriously wrong with Stalin. The leadership again repaired to the dacha, having called for medical help to be on hand. The doctors diagnosed a cerebral haemorrhage.

Khrushchev's account is contradicted in part by other reminiscences, but it is clear that Stalin did not receive any medical treatment for several hours after his stroke. Stalin was also paralysed down his right side and suffered loss of speech. This has led to speculation that the leadership was in no hurry to help him stay alive. Of the four top leaders Beria had the most to gain from the master's death. Both Khrushchev and Svetlana Alliluyeva record Beria's delight at Stalin's state. The latter regarded Beria's behaviour as 'obscene'. She blames him for poisoning her father's mind. Stalin died on 5 March 1953. During his last days his demeanour was that of an angry, embittered man. He was only capable of moving his little finger but it was clear what he was attempting to convey.

After Stalin's demise Beria almost danced with joy. Khrushchev and the others wept. Nikita Sergeevich says that his tears were partly for the state of the country and concern about the machinations of Beria in the near future.

PART TWO: DESCRIPTIVE ANALYSIS

2 BECOMING A STRONG NATIONAL LEADER, 1953–57

There were no rules or conventions about choosing a new Soviet leader. Stalin had ensured that there was no natural successor to him. However, since Malenkov had spoken for Stalin at the Nineteenth Party Congress he was regarded as the *Kronprinz*, the crown prince. All four wise men – Malenkov, Beria, Bulganin and Khrushchev – wanted to become another Stalin. This was not surprising, since he was the only role model they had. The immediate task for each was to ensure that the others did not succeed. Stalin's last illness allowed them time to fashion coalitions of interest. To Khrushchev, Beria presented the greatest danger, physically and politically. Khrushchev approached Bulganin and discovered that he also had misgivings about Lavrenty. Then he thought of speaking to Malenkov, but found out that Beria was a move ahead – he had already struck a deal with Malenkov. Even before Stalin was dead, during the night of 4–5 March 1953, the bureau of the Central Committee Presidium, consisting of Beria, Bulganin, Voroshilov, Kaganovich, Malenkov, Pervukhin, Saburov and Khrushchev, met and abolished the enlarged CC Presidium and the smaller bureau, and reverted to the usual Presidium. The next evening a joint session of the Central Committee, the USSR Council of Ministers and the Presidium of the USSR Supreme Soviet convened to confirm this decision and to decide on policy. The meeting ended at 8.40 p.m., or 70 minutes before Stalin died. At the meeting Malenkov and Beria took the initiative, confirming Khrushchev's worst fears. Beria nominated Malenkov as chairman of the Council of Ministers or Prime Minister, and Malenkov riposted by proposing Beria as one of his first deputies (together with Molotov, Bulganin and Kaganovich). Malenkov also proposed the fusing of the Ministries of Internal Affairs and State Security (MVD* and MGB*) into a unified Ministry of Internal Affairs, headed by Beria. Molotov regained his old position as foreign minister. Khrushchev nominated Bulganin as minister of defence.

When these arrangements were made public on 7 March there was also a plea for the public not to panic. This indicated how ill-at-ease the leadership was and the need to demonstrate a united front.

Khrushchev had to give up his post as first Party secretary of Moscow obkom, to 'concentrate on his duties in the CC Secretariat' (*Pravda*, 7 March 1953). During the first days after Stalin's death a cult of Malenkov's personality developed, with, for instance, a fabricated photograph of him appearing in *Pravda*. At the funeral speeches were made by Beria, Malenkov and Molotov. This appeared to be the new triumvirate. Beria was very disrespectful and did not bother to feign grief. Molotov was the most shaken by the master's death but both he and Malenkov spoke optimistically about the future. Nino, Beria's wife, observed that her husband 'had a practical mind and understood that it would be impossible for a Georgian to become leader after Stalin's death. Therefore he approached someone he could use, someone like Malenkov' [*65 p. 182*]. Beria and Malenkov became formidable political twins.

THE KEY POLITICAL INSTITUTION

A major problem was to identify the key political institution. Was it the USSR Council of Ministers or the Party Presidium? Was the Prime Minister a more powerful figure than the leader of the Party? It was not easy to answer these questions since there was no post which carried with it the headship of the Party. The position of secretary general had been abolished in 1934 and Stalin afterwards was addressed merely as a secretary of the CC. Because Lenin had been Prime Minister and Stalin had been in that post since 1941 there was a feeling that the head of government was also the key political actor. Whereas all the other members of the new Party Presidium occupied a government post, Khrushchev did not. He was the odd man out. Malenkov had inherited all three positions held by Stalin: Prime Minister, member of the Party Presidium and CC Secretariat*. He appeared to have donned the mantle of Stalin but this was deceptive since he had not acquired Stalin's power, only his positions. However, dissatisfaction was soon expressed that Malenkov had been invested with both top offices, head of government and head of the Party. On 14 March, the Presidium relieved Malenkov, 'at his own request', of his position in the CC Secretariat. As Khrushchev was the main beneficiary it can be assumed that he was behind the move. He was now the only person who was in the Presidium and the Secretariat. The Party now became his power base. As such his goal was to make the Party the primary institution in the state.

Khrushchev was a member of a collective leadership but the Soviet political system favoured the emergence of a strong national leader. The role models were Lenin and Stalin. Whereas Lenin became leader through his tactical and intellectual dominance, Stalin's power derived from crushing his political opponents. He maintained his power through cold-blooded ruthlessness and the ability to inspire and strike fear into his subordinates and the population. Lenin never aspired to become the dictator that Stalin became. It was unlikely that the new leader would possess either Lenin's intellectual dominance or Stalin's power.

BERIA

The nearest thing to a Stalin in the leadership was Beria. He was a master of intrigue, refined under Stalin, and was as deadly as a viper. He had, however, one weakness – arrogance. The civil and political police were his power base. He also commanded the border guards and ten MVD divisions. His men also guarded the Kremlin and all military weapons, including nuclear weapons. He made wholesale personnel changes in the internal and political police. The head of the foreign intelligence directorate was sacked and about 200 Soviet foreign agents were recalled to Moscow.

While a new leadership was settling in, it needed stability in the country. Thus concern for public opinion became important. The new regime needed to win over the population without resorting to violence. Beria, as a first deputy Prime Minister, immediately cancelled work on several high-profile projects, dear to Stalin's heart, which he regarded as a waste of resources. On 24 March, he presented a document to the Party Presidium which proposed an amnesty for a large number of prisoners. According to the document, of the 2,526,402 in labour camps, only 221,435 were 'especially dangerous state criminals'. The rest were not a threat to the state or the population. On 27 March, the Presidium approved a decree releasing all those serving sentences of up to five years, women with children under 10, pregnant women and those under 18. In all, around 1 million persons were freed [65 *p. 185*]. Times were now more relaxed, and it appeared that the long Stalin winter was coming to an end. The MVD – not the Ministry of Justice – announced that the Doctors' Plot (the arrest of Kremlin doctors in January 1953 on charges of having poisoned Andrei Zhdanov and other Soviet leaders) had been fabricated by deploying 'impermissible means of investigation'. All the doctors who were still alive were rehabilitated. Collective leadership was stressed and Stalin's name cited less and less. On 9 May, the Party Presidium, prompted by Beria, passed a resolution banning the appearance of leaders' portraits during festive demonstrations. Beria also made available to members of the Central Committee, in a special room in the Kremlin, documents implicating Stalin in the Doctors' Plot and showing how he had intended to use it against Beria.

Beria was acutely aware of the resentment felt by non-Russians at Russification as practised by Stalin and Stalin's men. Needless to say, Beria had been as ruthless as the next man in imposing this policy under Stalin. Now he reversed all the oppressive policies of 1951–52 in his native Georgia and installed his own nominees in Party and government. When he turned his attention to Ukraine he clashed head on with Khrushchev. Beria wanted ethnic Ukrainians promoted to the leadership and the use of the Ukrainian language when official business was being conducted. Particularly brutal Russification policies had been adopted in western Ukraine, annexed from Poland in 1939. Beria managed to get the Party Central Committee, on 26 May, to pass a resolution on western Ukraine which criticised the nationalities policy of the Communist Party of Ukraine and called for the dismissal of the ethnic Russian first secretary. He was duly removed and replaced by the Ukrainian Andrei Kirichenko. Beria, for the first time, became popular in Ukraine. Beria began the rehabilitation of the Uniate (Greek Catholic) Church in western Ukraine, which had been forced to merge with the Orthodox Church. He also promoted the normalisation of relations between Moscow and the Vatican.

All this turned Khrushchev's post-1945 policy in Ukraine on its head. Beria then concentrated on Belorussia, Lithuania, Latvia and Estonia, calling for the promotion of natives to top posts, the recall of ethnic Russian leaders to Moscow and the use of the local language in official affairs. As head of the MVD Beria had been replacing Russians everywhere with locals [65 *p. 189*]. Beria was sharply cognisant of another major problem bequeathed by Stalin, agriculture. He therefore proposed that peasants be permitted to cultivate more land for their own use and that collectivisation in the newly acquired territories – western Ukraine and the Baltic states, mainly – be slowed down.

Khrushchev could not really find fault with these policies. However, his reading of the motive behind Beria's nationality policy was that it was designed to foment trouble between Russians and non-Russians in the republics and between the republics and the Moscow centre.

THE EAST GERMAN CONFLICT

Khrushchev had a stroke of luck in foreign policy. The Soviet Union was pursuing *détente* and moved to end the war in Korea. The other major source of tension was divided Germany. In the Soviet Union Malenkov had promoted the New Course, which meant greater emphasis on consumer goods at the expense of heavy industry, and the East Germans, under Walter Ulbricht, were encouraged to do the same. However, the East German regime had launched an ambitious programme of industrialisation and forced collectivisation in 1952 and opposition was such that hundreds of thousands of East Germans were voting with their feet and moving to West Germany. Ulbricht asked for economic aid at Stalin's funeral and afterwards, but the Kremlin responded by advising him to slow down the pace of socialist construction. Instead, in mid-May the East German leadership increased industrial work norms by 10 per cent without any compensation. On 27 May, the Presidium of the USSR Council of Ministers met to discuss the situation in the GDR. A document, drafted and signed by Beria, was agreed on 2 June. It recommended that the East German leadership abandon the forced construction of socialism; promote the establishment of a united, democratic, peace-loving and independent Germany; abandon forced collectivisation which peasants opposed strongly; attract private capital into the economy; improve the financial system; end the unjust and cruel judicial treatment of citizens and review the cases of those already sentenced [*65 p. 191*]. Ulbricht and two other members of the Politburo of the SED – the Socialist Unity Party of Germany (the ruling communist party in the GDR) – who were in Moscow from 2 to 4 June, were obliged to accept this document. It was then adopted by the SED Politburo as a whole. On 10 June the SED Politburo duly made known its New Course, but the 10 per cent increase in labour norms remained. The Russian newspaper in East Germany then criticised the Soviet Military Control Commission for having committed serious errors. Beria was working through Rudolf Herrnstadt, editor of *Neues Deutschland*, the Party newspaper, and Wilhelm Zaisser, the Minister of National Security – and directly subordinate to Beria – to replace Ulbricht with a more liberal leader. This might have succeeded had not the workers intervened. On 16 June, East Berlin workers took to the streets, and on the next day the uprising spread to many parts of the German Democratic Republic (GDR). The Soviets intervened with tanks on 17 June and communist power was saved. Khrushchev seized the initiative to blame Beria for this dangerous turn of events, accusing him of forcing reforms on the East German leadership and of contemplating abandoning the GDR.

THE DOWNFALL OF BERIA

Khrushchev was the driving force in the conspiracy against Beria, which came to a head when the latter was arrested at a Party Presidium meeting on 26 June 1953. Khrushchev already had Bulganin on his side, and by extension many in the military. Malenkov held the key, and Khrushchev worked to undermine his commitment to Beria. He got Malenkov to draft Presidium motions which would result in policy defeats for Beria, and in this way made clear to Malenkov that the Georgian could be outmanoeuvred. Beria sensed what was going on and lobbied Molotov, but Molotov had gone over to Khrushchev during the East German crisis.

> Beria called me and asked me to support his group. I told him on the contrary, he should support our position. But he would not listen, and hung up on me. He thought it would be easy to get even with Khrushchev's group, but Khrushchev turned out to be more clever. If Beria had listened to me, history would have had a different outcome [65 p. 195].

Molotov had a high opinion of Beria. 'Beria was a most clever man, inhumanly energetic and industrious. He could work for a week without sleep' [65 p. 195]. Voroshilov was a great Beria admirer, as was Mikoyan. Kaganovich was out of town. Khrushchev convinced Malenkov, Molotov and Bulganin to take the lead. All MVD troops were loyal to Beria, so it would be a major problem to arrest him. Khrushchev's solution was to hand-pick top military officers whom he knew from the war and promise them promotion or awards.

The whole operation was launched suddenly, on the evening of 25 June. The next morning Khrushchev recruited General Moskalenko, commander of Moscow's air defences, and he in turn recruited others. Marshal Zhukov joined the conspiracy. When the Presidium meeting began Beria was taken aback by Khrushchev berating him for past mistakes. He was followed by Bulganin and then Molotov.

Malenkov, in the chair, was then supposed to summarise the charges. However, he lost his nerve and was struck dumb. Thereupon Khrushchev proposed that Beria be relieved of all his posts, but Malenkov, instead of putting the motion to a vote, got in a panic and pressed the wrong button, summoning the military officers. Marshal Zhukov and others then burst in and arrested Beria. However, it was one thing to arrest him, it was another to get him out of the Kremlin, still guarded by his men, and into prison. They managed to do so late in the evening and conveyed him to Lefortovo prison, where, ironically, Beria had maltreated many prisoners. The leadership feared the use of military force to free Beria but no attack was attempted. His wife and son were also imprisoned.

Because the Presidium had no authority to arrest Beria, they declared him an enemy of the Party and the people. A secret plenary meeting of the Central Committee (the stenographic records were only made available in 1991) met from 2 to 7 July 1953 to pass judgement on Beria. It was a hazardous operation since no motion had been put to the vote in the Presidium on 26 June. Khrushchev and his co-conspirators were skating on thin ice as they presented the arrest as a *fait accompli* to the CC. Molotov revealed that Beria had been conducting foreign policy through the MVD and that a letter had been written to Alexander (*sic*) Rankovich in which Beria requested a secret meeting with him and Tito so as to normalise Soviet – Yugoslav relations (Stalin had expelled Yugoslavia from the Cominform in June 1948.) Molotov revealed that the letter had been found in Beria's briefcase when arrested and this proved that he was an 'agent of the class enemy' [65 p. 206]. Bulganin claimed that Beria was a spy who had been collecting information on the Soviet Union's armed forces to pass on to the enemy. Kaganovich, who does not appear to have known about the conspiracy beforehand, weighed in by condemning Beria for being involved in a 'dangerous, counter-revolutionary, adventurous plot against the Party and government' [65 p. 206]. Speaker after speaker was called to damn Beria. Eventually Mikoyan was called and he toed the line by providing some more damning evidence and repeating the usual claims that Beria had been a spy. The Party was being prepared for the charge of treason which would bring the death sentence. Some light relief was introduced by a CC secretary who reported on the results of a search of Beria's office. Women's clothes, letters and so on said much about his relations with women, and his former bodyguard provided a long list of women with whom Beria had been enjoying sexual relations. It could also be proved that he was the father of several illegitimate children and had syphilis. Charges that he had kidnapped young girls, given them a sleeping drug and then raped them, were first levied at his trial.

Speakers contradicted one another at the plenum, revealing how little time there had been for preparation. Khrushchev wanted to concentrate fire on Beria's early career and his activities since March 1953. He expressly wished to exclude any mention of the years 1937 and 1938 when Beria had been the butcher of Georgia and elsewhere, since all members of the leadership shared Beria's guilt for the purges. Khrushchev maintained that Beria had been conspiring to seize power and had been caught in the act. Konstantin Simonov, who attended the plenum, wrote:

> It was completely obvious to me when I listened to him that Khrushchev was the initiator of this red-handed catch, because he was shrewder, more talented, energetic and decisive than the others. On the other hand, he was helped by the fact that Beria underestimated Khrushchev, his qualities – his deeply natural, pure masculinity, his tenacious cunning, his common sense and his strength of character. Beria, on the contrary, considered Khrushchev a round-headed fool, whom Beria, the master of intrigue, could wrap around his finger [65 *p. 209*].

The CC voted for a resolution calling for Beria's expulsion from the Party and his trial on criminal charges. *Pravda* revealed the conclusions of the plenum on 10 July. A CC letter to lower Party bodies stated that the Presidium had unmasked Beria as an 'agent of international imperialism'. Party activists at all levels were ordered to hold meetings to denounce Beria, since the leadership was very uncertain about rank-and-file reaction. Indeed, many expressed doubts about the charges against Beria, and in Moscow Party workers asked many questions and did not appear to believe the official line [65 *p. 211*].

Local Party leaders were informed of the indictment against Beria and six accomplices on 15 December 1953. Two days later the USSR Procurator General announced that investigations were at an end and that the trial would soon begin. It was held in camera from 18 to 23 December. It was a political trial; no pretence was made about following judicial procedures. Rumours still persist, despite the forty volumes of evidence collected and the transcripts of the trial, that Beria was executed in late June or early July 1953 and not in December. The whole episode was a Stalinist operation. Beria was too dangerous to the living so he had to die.

Many of Beria's policies were later adopted by Khrushchev, who proved himself a good political magpie. They included de-Stalinisation, concessions to the peasants and the republics, and the normalisation of relations with Yugoslavia. Indeed, Beria's perception that East Germany was a liability was finally conceded by Gorbachev. His promotion of national elites in the republics pre-dated similar efforts by Andropov and Gorbachev. Had he remained in power it is possible that his pragmatic policies would have had quite an impact. Like Gorbachev, he might not have succeeded in solving the intractable problems of Soviet power, but had he tried, the world almost certainly would have been different. In sum, Germany was the greatest loser.

THE REHABILITATIONS BEGIN

The MVD apparatus was the greatest barrier to the re-establishment of the dominance of the Communist Party. Khrushchev now had the opportunity to promote the claims of the Presidium and Central Committee. However, he had to be mindful of the fact that the Council of Ministers was a powerful institution, as over half the members of the Presidium were ministers. Beria in death was useful to Khrushchev. He had spewed out much material which could later be used against Malenkov and the others. This material would have to be used sparingly, as everyone in the leadership had a vested interest in the Party being economical with the truth. They had all participated in heinous events. A cautious start was made on rehabilitating the innocent, but it only affected the elite, their families and friends. About 1,000 had been rehabilitated (some posthumously) by the end of 1953. One of those who returned to Moscow was Lyubov Khrushcheva, the widow of Leonid, Khrushchev's son. He had been killed in aerial combat in 1943 near Voronezh, but his body was never found as his plane had crashed into a bog. Lyubov had been arrested and condemned as a Swedish spy. Another was Molotov's wife, and the accusations that she had spied for the United States and Israel (she was a Jewess) were dropped. In normal circumstances, if the wife of a minister of foreign affairs had been found guilty of spying for the 'great, imperialist enemy', the United States, it would also have ended his career. Perhaps Stalin wanted to play cat and mouse with Molotov. On one occasion he told him that he had been reliably informed that he was a Jew. Usually Molotov could get out about one sentence before he began to stammer. On this occasion he fluently replied: 'Oh, no, Comrade Stalin, you have been misinformed.' Whereupon Stalin countered: 'Vyacheslav Mikhailovich, I would think it over, if I were you!' [77 p. 37].

MALENKOV VERSUS KHRUSHCHEV

Beria's removal brought the first round of the Kremlin contest to find the next strong national leader to an end. The second round would be between Malenkov and his allies, and Khrushchev and his allies. Malenkov's power base was the government and Khrushchev's the Party. The latter quickly revealed his common touch. Stalin had turned the Kremlin into a fortress (quite appropriate, as 'kremlin' means fortress in Russian) because of his fear (probably quite justified) of assassination. No one was allowed in without a special pass. Even photographing it was prohibited. Towards the end of 1953, however, it was reopened to the public. All that was needed was a ticket. A New Year's Ball was inaugurated for young people and a Christmas tree put up for the children.

Control over the civil and political police after Beria's departure was of supreme importance. The Ministry of Internal Affairs (MVD) was again split into two. Civil and criminal offences were to be the responsibility of the new MVD, and a newly created Committee (not Ministry) of State Security (KGB)* was to oversee state security at home and abroad. A subtle change was introduced. Whereas previously all orders stemmed from Beria, now the guards were to receive their instructions from the person they were guarding. Khrushchev had a say in the appointment of the new KGB chief, General Ivan Serov. He knew him well from his Ukrainian days, when he had been People's Commissar for Internal Affairs, and trusted him: 'I thought and still think him to be an honest man where the Party is concerned. And if there is something "on him", as is the case with all Chekists, so to speak, well, he was in that respect a victim of the general policy that Stalin pursued' [57 p. 98]. However, Serov had an unsavoury reputation, and when he visited London ahead of Khrushchev and Bulganin in 1956 the tabloids savaged him and he had to be recalled. Khrushchev did not know Kruglov, the MVD chief, personally. Revealingly, this meant that Khrushchev did not trust him. The USSR Procurator General became the supreme law enforcement officer in the Soviet Union, as did his counterpart at republican level, with all being subordinate to him. The notorious Special Boards, under which the political police had had the power to sentence defendants in their absence, were phased out. Of course, all this did not transform the Soviet Union into a *Rechtsstaat,* where the rule of law prevailed. However, it did begin the process of the rehabilitation of socialist law. Socialist legality would still be defined by the supreme Party agency, the Presidium.

Khrushchev revealed more daring, enterprise and skill than Malenkov. A prime area was personnel. The Soviet system was based on the *nomenklatura**, which was a list both of all key positions and of available individuals to fill them. Each official attempted to build up a 'tail' of loyal subordinates, and as he moved upwards many of his subordinates moved up as well. They, in turn, grew 'tails'. The upwardly mobile politician was like a growing tree. Since the other members of the Party and state elites were trying simultaneously to expand their 'tails', considerable skill was needed to place one's men and a few women in positions of minor and major influence. Nikita Sergeevich began with a great advantage: he was *de facto* head of the Party. However, this was not enough. He had to promote policies which promised to move the country forward politically, economically and socially. Then there was the need to strike tactical political coalitions in order gradually to downgrade political opponents. Above all, he needed some luck. If Malenkov's economic policies had been brilliantly successful Khrushchev might not have climbed to the top of the political pole. Needless to say, he was not going to do anything to make Georgy Maksimilianovich a political or economic success.

It took Khrushchev until February 1955, when Malenkov resigned as Prime Minister, to get the better of his arch rival. After Stalin's death Nikita Sergeevich was just one member of the political elite. Then he became *de facto* Party leader. He rose to be *primus inter pares* (first among equals) when Malenkov stepped down as Prime Minister, but he did not become a strong national leader until July 1957. Technically he was only Party leader in July 1957, and in order to rise to strong national leader he needed a great office of state. Although he took over as Prime Minister, replacing Nikolai Bulganin in March 1958, in effect he had been head of government since the summer of 1957. Bulganin had been a member of the Anti-Party group defeated by Khrushchev and had stayed in office mainly for the sake of appearances. The Yugoslav ambassador, Micunovic, relates that he advised against the demotion of Bulganin in July 1957, since those abroad might construe such a move by Khrushchev as evidence that he was just another Stalinist hood. By the summer of 1958 Khrushchev had emulated his mentor, Stalin. It took him five years to do so, the same period Iosif Vissarionovich had needed after Lenin's death in 1924. Stalin's task had been immeasurably more difficult. Nikita Sergeevich had not had to outmanoeuvre such hugely talented comrades as Trotsky and Bukharin. It requires considerable imagination to conceive of Nikita Sergeevich getting the better of these two, given that he did not consider killing one's political opponents as one of the rules of the game.

Stalin had done Khrushchev a favour. All the clever men had been eliminated from the top echelons of Party and state power with no new ones to take their place. One can coin the expression 'the law of diminishing brain power'. The brilliant Lenin was followed by the crafty Stalin, who killed intellectual debate at the top. Then came Khrushchev, who only had a limited grasp of Marxism. He was followed by Brezhnev, who preferred flattery to hard thinking (he was known as 'the ballerina': his head could be turned in any direction). Andropov was never well enough to make an impact. The depths were plumbed by the election of Chernenko. Perhaps one should not be too harsh on him. He could hardly speak. The arrival of Gorbachev was the exception which proved the rule. However, in the end, he destroyed the system. The limited intellectual ability of so many leaders had a catastrophic effect on the way the country was managed. Moreover, the expansion of education had produced many highly talented, educated people in every walk of life. There could not be a debate between leaders and led because the leaders could not prevail in such a debate. The result was a loss of political authority by the leaders. Another by-product was that violent quarrels were bound to break out between the intelligentsia (educated and white-collar workers) and the guardians of political orthodoxy. The latter's view reflected the past and favoured the *status quo*, whereas creative minds wanted to move forward. Khrushchev inevitably was to be caught up in this struggle and to side with the orthodox officials. Only in retirement did he see the error of his ways.

KHRUSHCHEV AND COERCION

Khrushchev elected not to apply one of the rules of the political game at which Stalin was a past master: coercion. Nikita Sergeevich abjured the use of force for political gain after Beria had been disposed of. This made his task as a runner in the race to become a strong national leader all the more difficult. As late as July 1957 his defeated opponents expected to suffer physically as well as politically for their defeat. It also made his hold on power less secure, since opponents became more bold in opposing those policies which they deemed inimical to their interests. What were the rules of the political game in the Soviet Union and how did the resourceful mind of Khrushchev apply them?

KHRUSHCHEV AND HIS 'TAIL'

As he was head of the CC Secretariat Khrushchev could place his nominees in key Party posts and infiltrate the government network, where he was weak. *De facto* head in March, he became *de jure* head in September 1953 when he was elected First Secretary of the CC of the Communist Party of the Soviet Union. This was a new post, as Stalin had been Secretary General until 1934. The new title was to stress the break with the past. In 1966, Brezhnev had himself renamed Secretary General. There were five main types of official whom Khrushchev attempted to add to his 'tail':

1 those who had served successfully under him in Ukraine and Moscow;
2 those whose patrons had lost ground in the leadership struggle, such as Beria's men after July 1953 and Malenkov's entourage after February 1955;
3 those who had been Stalin's men until his death and then had lost out to the aspirations of Malenkov, Beria, Molotov and their 'tails';
4 those who had been the losers in the factional in-fighting of the late Stalin era – e.g., the Leningrad Affair; and
5 bright, capable, young officials who could be promoted over the heads of their superiors.

The group which fared best after Khrushchev entered the Secretariat were, not surprisingly, those who had been in his team in Ukraine and Moscow. Many of them became first Party secretaries at *oblast* and *krai** levels, and others moved into the central Party apparatus in Moscow. Recruits from groups (3) and (4) promised to be loyal since they were resentful of Beria and Malenkov. One informed estimate is that by the Twentieth Party Congress in February 1956

Khrushchev's Ukrainian and Moscow supporters, and others listed above, constituted about a third of the full members of the CC. By the end of 1957, after consolidating his victory over the Anti-Party group, Nikita Sergeevich's team from the above groups made up the overwhelming majority of full CC members. Besides cultivating his 'tail' in Moscow, Khrushchev was quietly doing the same in the republican Communist Parties. Each of the fifteen republics had its own Communist Party except the Russian Federation, which had to wait until 1990. Republican parties were closely supervised from the centre. It is reasonable to assume that Khrushchev's orbit of patronage embraced republican, *oblast* and *krai* government leaders, top-flight police officers and officials in agricultural ministries. However, the majority of senior posts in the central state apparatus were still beyond his reach.

KHRUSHCHEV AND THE ECONOMY

The Stalinist command economy (so called because it was based on commands or orders from the centre), referred to as the 'command-administrative system' under Gorbachev, had concentrated great power in the central governmental ministries. Since Khrushchev's main Presidium opponents had their power bases in these ministries, there was little he could do if the economy continued to function as before. Criticisms of the performance of industry and agriculture at the July 1953 plenum afforded him the opportunity of proposing reforms. Whole industries were regarded as backward. Industry was not able to supply agriculture with enough equipment and to satisfy the 'material and cultural' needs of the population (this was a code conceding that living standards were low). It occurred to Khrushchev that if economic decision-making could be decentralised it would help him in two ways. It would undermine the political bases of his challengers and, because there was no intention to move to a market economy, an organisation would be needed to allocate resources and control, coordinate and resolve the conflicts which would inevitably arise. The obvious organisation to perform these functions was the Communist Party. Its apparatus would gradually become more influential than that of the government. The *nomenklatura* system would facilitate the placing of the right people in government and local authority or soviet jobs.

Khrushchev was surprisingly successful in devolving decision-making to the republics, given that his political opponents must have been aware of the long-term aim of this reform. In 1954–55 approximately 11,000 enterprises were transferred from central to republican control. In May 1955, many major planning and financial decisions, hitherto taken in Moscow, were devolved to republican governments. In May 1956, enterprises run by twelve central government ministries were placed under the jurisdiction of republican bodies. Then, in May 1957, over a hundred Councils of the National Economy (*sovnarkhozy**) were established, thereby eliminating the central economic ministries. Ministries involved in the defence sector were exempt. It was only when Khrushchev pushed through the *sovnarkhoz* reform that the Presidium majority revolted. It was now quite clear what Nikita Sergeevich's objective was. His opponents were labelled the Anti-Party group, meaning that they had resisted the predominance of the Party in economic decision-making. They wanted the government to run the economy. The Party's major role in economic affairs lasted until 1988 when Gorbachev unceremoniously deprived the Party apparatus of this key function.

DEMOCRATISATION

Khrushchev needed policy issues in order to challenge Malenkov effectively. The latter and Beria had launched the New Course after Stalin's death and promised a rise in living standards by switching resources from heavy to light industry and the intensification of agriculture. What became known as 'democratisation' under Gorbachev – more discussion at the grass roots but under firm central direction – was launched. East European Communist Parties were encouraged to follow suit, but most resisted. The East German leadership had to be ordered to toe the line, but it resisted and the June uprising occurred. The others were as conservative, but all they achieved was the postponement of the crisis until 1956.

AGRICULTURE

The virgin lands

Domestically, Khrushchev had to respond to Malenkov's and Beria's initiatives. Malenkov was stronger on industrial than rural affairs. Fortunately for Nikita Sergeevich, his strengths were the reverse. At the Nineteenth Party Congress in 1952, Malenkov had given a hostage to fortune by declaring that the grain problem 'in the main had been solved'. This was based on the estimated yields of standing grain, called the biological yield, which were about one-third higher than what actually ended up in the barn. It was a simple matter to demonstrate that Malenkov was wrong. In September 1953, Khrushchev launched a major shake-up of the procurement system. The quickest way to increase output was to encourage peasants to grow more on their private plots. Taxes and compulsory delivery quotas were therefore reduced, and peasants were provided with more pastureland and fodder for their own livestock. Payments in kind for work on the kolkhoz (or collective farm) and the sovkhoz (or state farm) were increased. Farms were to be paid more for compulsory deliveries to the state. Everyone agreed that a rapid increase in grain output was necessary. This would, in turn, provide more fodder and consequently more milk and meat products. Khrushchev called on farmers to sow more, harvest more, eat more, but how was he to obtain control over the implementation of this policy?

The central agricultural ministries were under the control of his opponents, and the farms were not subordinate to him. In September he managed to make the *raion* Party secretary and his assistants, centred in the Machine Tractor Stations (MTS), the chief supervisors of the implementation of agrarian policy in the kolkhozes. At that time farms did not possess enough machinery since there was not enough to go round. The agricultural departments of the *raion* soviets were abolished. This weakened the links between the farms and the agricultural agencies and central government. Information about the rural sector gradually fell within the orbit of the Party and this made Khrushchev the best-informed person on rural affairs. The reform was an astute political move but of doubtful economic value. This arrangement lasted until 1958, when the MTS were abolished and machinery was sold, or more accurately off-loaded, to the farms. There was no longer any need to administer agriculture from the MTS, since by then the *raion* first Party secretary had established his authority. Another reason was that Khrushchev became Prime Minister in 1958 and hence head of the governmental administration.

Given that agricultural production in 1953 only grew by 2.5 per cent (industrial production claimed a 12 per cent rise), there was an urgent need to increase food output. Khrushchev knew that there were millions of hectares of virgin (previously untilled) and idle (previously cultivated and since abandoned) land throughout the country. However, much of it was marginal (of doubtful economic value) and located in dry farming zones (very low annual precipitation) where special techniques are needed to preserve the fertility of the soil. In February 1954 hundreds of thousands of Komsomol* members from Moscow city and *oblast* assembled in the capital. Khrushchev and A. I. Benediktov, the Minister of Agriculture, appealed to the young people to participate in the opening up of the virgin and idle lands. Since there would be few creature comforts in west Siberia, north Kazakhstan, the Urals and the north Caucasus, the imagination of the young people had to be fired. The older generation preferred to stay at home. There were doubters in the Party Presidium, especially Molotov, who preferred intensification (more from the same area). Khrushchev countered by claiming that that would be expensive and would only produce results slowly. His initiative would be cheaper – recouping costs in two or three years, one of his favourite expressions – and would produce results very quickly. Perhaps his political opponents thought they were giving him enough rope to hang himself. He very nearly did.

The Kazakhs were not enamoured of the idea at all. North Kazakhstan was a traditional livestock grazing area. Ploughing it up would attract a flood of Russians, Ukrainians and others, thus making the Kazakhs, already a minority in their own republic, even worse off. Khrushchev sacked the Kazakh Party leadership and installed his own. The comrade chosen to be second secretary was Leonid Brezhnev, who soon became first secretary. By the end of February 1954 thousands of young enthusiasts were on their way to Siberia and Kazakhstan. Few of them had any experience of farming, let alone dry farming, and they had no tools. Only the most perfunctory of surveys had been carried out in Kazakhstan. The need for more food was so great that will-power took over. It was reminiscent of the 1930s.

A CC plenum in February 1954 approved Khrushchev's proposal to plough up 13 million hectares of virgin land, which was expected to yield 20 million tonnes of grain in 1955. This was very ambitious, but Nikita Sergeevich was a 100 per cent politician and he was convinced that the virgin lands were the new Eldorado for the Soviet Union. State farms had to be set up, since no one at present farmed there. A CC plenum in May 1954 heard another wonder solution: the cultivation of maize. It would solve the fodder problem at a stroke. Khrushchev did not pretend that the average peasant would agree with him, so he requested that the sowing of maize be made mandatory everywhere. Coercion was appropriate wherever necessary; after all, peasants had refused to believe that potatoes were good for them in the eighteenth century! It was judged politic not to publish the section about coercion. Khrushchev's passion for maize – it is a valuable crop in Ukraine but rarely ripens elsewhere – earned him the sobriquet Comrade Kukuruznik (from the Russian for maize, *kukuruza*). It was not intended to be complimentary. So keen was Khrushchev on the crop that he grew it at his dacha in Moscow. With the virgin lands producing more grain, this would free other regions, such as Ukraine, to grow maize for fodder. In 1957 Khrushchev promised that the Soviet Union would catch up with the United States in the production of milk, butter and meat. However, this would have involved tripling meat production – an impossible task.

Other Agricultural Initiatives

Agricultural production was officially stated to have increased by only 3 per cent in 1954. The food problem had still to be solved. Another CC plenum in January 1955 launched a livestock plan, and procurement prices rose again. In March 1955, the Minister of State Farms was sacked and replaced by Benediktov, the Minister of Agriculture. The new Minister of Agriculture was Vladimir Matskevich, a specialist in animal husbandry, whom Khrushchev knew from his Ukrainian days.

Nikita Sergeevich continued his policy of amalgamating kolkhozes. Over the period 1953 to 1958 their numbers dropped from over 90,000 to under 70,000 and declined rapidly thereafter. There were two reasons for this. Large units were regarded as more effective, and in 1953 very few farms had a primary Party organisation. More than 20,000 technical specialists were sent from the cities to the MTS and farms. As a result over 90 per cent of kolkhoz chairmen by 1958 were communists (Party members) and the average kolkhoz had a primary Party organisation of about twenty members. There had to be incentives to raise production. By the end of the Stalin era most farms were operating at a loss, since procurement prices, which were set by the state, had hardly increased since 1928. In the period 1953–57 they almost tripled. The policy of expanding the sown area was pursued with vigour. Over the years 1954–60 a staggering 41.8 million hectares of virgin and idle land were ploughed, with west Siberia and northern Kazakhstan contributing about three-quarters. However, in 1960 the increase in the sown area was only 30 million hectares. State procurement of grain rose by almost 50 per cent annually between

1954 and 1963, with most of the increase coming from the virgin lands. However, the cost of growing this extra grain was very high. The Soviet Union refused to import grain for domestic consumption before 1963. Grain at any price was preferable to famine, and more grain meant more fodder.

How was it that Khrushchev was able to play such an innovative role in agriculture as well as influencing industrial decision-making? After Stalin's death it was uncertain where the centre of legitimacy in the Soviet state lay. Khrushchev sedulously cultivated the view that the Party Central Committee was the key institution. Between March 1953 and July 1957 the CC played a role reminiscent of that of the latter part of the 1920s. After Lenin's death Stalin enjoyed more support in the CC than the Politburo. Hence he concentrated debate in it, and appealed to it if Politburo members rejected his policies. However, when Stalin achieved ascendancy in 1929, the CC declined in significance. During the last six years of the master's life it only met in plenary session twice. Membership merely confirmed a comrade's standing. According to Party rules the CC is the supreme Party body, and it soon became normal for every major shift in policy among the elite to be confirmed by a CC plenum. The first division of power after Stalin's death, Beria's arrest, Khrushchev's appointment as First Secretary and Malenkov's dismissal as Prime Minister, were all endorsed by a CC plenum. Another reason for this was the uncertainty felt by the leadership about rank-and-file Party reaction, as well as that of the population at large, to their policies. Because Nikita Sergeevich held no government office, the only way he could propagate his agricultural views was by convening a CC plenum. Being head of the Secretariat made this easy. Another tactic was to forward a memorandum to Presidium members. Only those present knew precisely what Khrushchev was proposing. Most of his speeches at this time were only published in 1962. His use of the CC plenum transformed it into a body which participated in the formation of policy. Enormous publicity attended the meetings, and the proceedings were later published, a major innovation, harking back again to the early years of Soviet power. CC plenums were convened in September 1953 to launch Khrushchev's agricultural policy; in February 1954 to begin the virgin lands campaign; in June 1954, again on the virgin lands; and in January 1955 to propagate his livestock policy.

Map 1 The USSR *c.* 1960

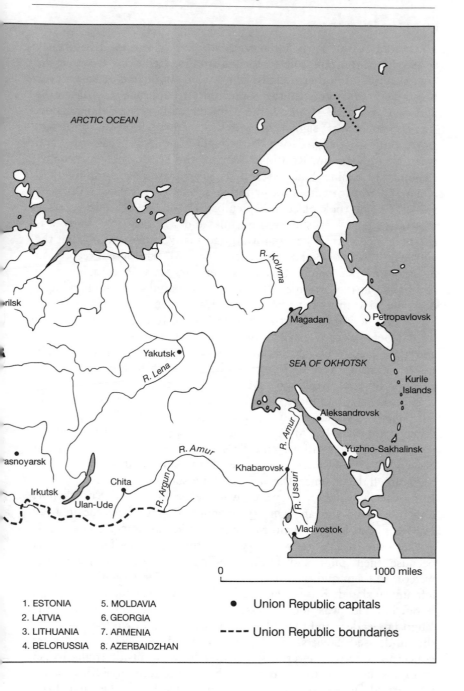

1. ESTONIA   5. MOLDAVIA
2. LATVIA   6. GEORGIA
3. LITHUANIA 7. ARMENIA
4. BELORUSSIA 8. AZERBAIDZHAN

● Union Republic capitals

---- Union Republic boundaries

FOREIGN POLICY

The resurgence of Party influence made it possible for Khrushchev to play an important role in foreign affairs. Relations between the Soviet Union and other socialist states were conducted at Party level. Nikita Sergeevich grasped the opportunity to upgrade the role of the Party and to push Molotov, the Minister of Foreign Affairs, aside. An armistice was signed in Korea in July 1953. In 1954 an agreement was signed which brought about a cease-fire and partition in Vietnam. Relations between the USSR and the People's Republic of China had never been very fraternal, as Stalin had attempted to turn China into another satellite. However, an official visit to Beijing took place in September 1954. The Soviet delegation was headed by Khrushchev, Bulganin and Mikoyan. Molotov was left at home. Khrushchev and Mao had many conversations, but the wily Mao bamboozled Khrushchev [*Doc. 8*]. The latter records in his memoirs that some of Mao's statements were so complex as to be opaque in the extreme. Others were so banal as to be blindingly obvious. Mao must have been very pleased, since he got practically everything he bid for. Port Arthur was to be returned to China and the Soviets were to hand over their share of jointly owned enterprises. A flood of specialists from the USSR, and eventually eastern Europe, were to be sent to build socialism there. It was all give and no take. No wonder Molotov had been left at home.

Yugoslavia was a more daunting task. Conventional wisdom held that Tito's regime was a 'military-fascist dictatorship', but now things improved. *Pravda* began to say nice things about Soviet–Yugoslav relations and Tass described them as 'cordial' in November 1954, after the Soviet leadership had turned up to celebrate Independence Day at the Yugoslav embassy in Moscow. Just how cordial they were was revealed when Khrushchev, Bulganin, Mikoyan and Dmitry Shepilov flew to Belgrade in May 1955 to mend fences. Again Molotov was left at home.

The Soviet delegation was very thankful to set foot on terra firma because their pilot had found landing difficult. Tito [*Doc. 12*] welcomed them and then ordered that Nikita Sergeevich's speech be left untranslated. Khrushchev blamed all the misunderstandings on Beria, but Tito was not impressed. At the subsequent reception the Yugoslav leaders and their elegant ladies looked down their noses at the ill-dressed Soviets. As far as Nikita Sergeevich's suits were concerned one was never sure whether he was outside trying to get in or inside trying to get out. At the return reception Khrushchev got carried away and imbibed too much: 'He had to be carried out

between rows of diplomats and other guests on the arms of Tito and
Rankovic, with his feet sketching out the motions of walking
without ever touching the ground' [76 *p. 217*]. Sir Frank Roberts,
the British Ambassador, observed the visit. Khrushchev's handling of
the Yugoslav question was typical of his approach to so many of the
problems he was convinced he could solve:

> He started with a brainwave, calling for rapid action alien to the
> thought processes of his more plodding colleagues and running
> risks of failure and even humiliation, but which, if successful,
> could bring big dividends and realise important policy objectives.
> His impulsive handling of the situation was clumsy and
> counter-productive, but he then retrieved from the apparent wreck
> enough of his original purpose to justify the enterprise [76 *p.
> 217*].

Khrushchev was very keen to restore inter-Party relations with the
Yugoslavs and welcome them back as the prodigal son to the
socialist commonwealth. Tito had no intention of conceding
primacy to the CPSU*, especially since Nikita Sergeevich always
maintained that his Party knew best, but he was willing to restore
inter-state relations and to lean in the direction of the Soviet Union
from time to time. For example, Tito sided with Khrushchev during
the Hungarian Revolution in 1956. The West began to perceive that
the Stalinist mould was being broken and that serious negotiations
could begin with the Soviets. One of the first fruits of this was the
Austrian Peace Treaty of May 1955. Molotov, predictably, objected
to the Soviet concessions. Soviet troops left the country voluntarily,
the first time this had happened since 1945, and Austria became a
neutral state. This heralded a change in Soviet thinking. Hitherto
Moscow had hoped that partitioned Austria and Germany would
fall into their lap. Now they realised this was not going to happen
and struck a deal on Austria.

The Warsaw Pact, the socialist riposte to NATO, also came into
being in May 1955. The original draft, prepared by Molotov, did
not contain Yugoslavia, of course, but it also omitted the German
Democratic Republic and Albania. The reason for leaving Albania
out was that it was 'far away' and had no common frontier with the
Soviet Union. As for the GDR, Molotov simply asked: 'Why should
we fight with the west over the GDR?' [77 *p. 52*]. Khrushchev
pointed out that if these two countries were omitted it would be
tantamount to handing them over to the West. This view prevailed

and they were included. The first summit meeting since Potsdam took place in Geneva in July 1955 [*Doc. 13*]. President Eisenhower headed the US delegation. Khrushchev, Bulganin, Molotov and Marshal Zhukov represented the Soviet Union, but Molotov did not take part in any of the substantive discussions. Khrushchev got on very well with Edgar Faure, the head of the French delegation, calling him Edgar Fedorovich. The Geneva spirit gave rise to a communiqué which spoke of the possibility of all-German elections. However, on his way home Nikita Sergeevich dropped in on Ulbricht in East Berlin and assured him that this would only happen with his consent – which, of course, was never forthcoming. This marked a shift in policy on the part of the Soviet leadership, which was now, for the first time, committed to two German states.

In a 'strictly secret' letter to Walter Ulbricht, dated 14 July 1955, Khrushchev informed him that the decision had been taken to release all German prisoners-of-war and civilians who were still being held in the Soviet Union. This was to include war criminals. Moscow was preparing the ground for negotiations to establish diplomatic relations with Bonn. The chief goal of the Soviets was to establish beneficial trade links. Chancellor Adenauer of West Germany tried to 'buy' the GDR from Moscow by offering generous credits and reparations, but Khrushchev resisted the temptation. He remarked: 'Once you start retreating, it's hard to stop' [77 *p. 53*]. The prisoners were released a week after Adenauer's visit to Moscow.

American efforts in 1954–55 to widen the ring of containment around the Soviet Union by recruiting countries on its southern periphery – Pakistan, Iran and Iraq – made Moscow very nervous. The Soviets were encouraged by the hostile reception that US policy encountered in much of the Third World (the First World was the United States and its allies; the Second World was the USSR and eastern Europe; the Third World was the rest) and this encouraged Moscow to cultivate countries there. In October 1955, U Nu, the Burmese leader, visited Moscow, and the following month Khrushchev and Bulganin travelled to Burma, India and Afghanistan. The Indian trip might have been their last. So great was the crush on one occasion that their official car was taken to pieces by the crowds, and they had to be passed overhead by their security guards to safety. Their tour made headline news throughout the world.

The Soviet Union's standing in the world was boosted enormously in December 1955 by the explosion of its second massive thermonuclear device at high altitude. Moscow now had a transportable hydrogen bomb which was more destructive than any American weapon, and was firmly in the big league [*Doc. 4*]. Nikita Sergeevich was fascinated by rockets and weaponry and took an almost childish delight in discussing their design with scientists and engineers. Rather like a child with a new toy, he could not resist boasting that his rockets were better than anyone else's. This was later to have unfortunate side effects and to trigger an escalation of the arms race, as the Americans took his braggadocio seriously. The Khrushchev–Bulganin double act reached London in April 1956 (they became known as B & K) [*Doc. 14*]. Nikita Sergeevich found the trip enormously stimulating and met, among others, the Queen and Sir Winston Churchill. When he mentioned that the process of change was very complex, the veteran British politician advised him to be bold. 'Any delay could result in the most serious consequences. It is like crossing a precipice. One may leap over it, if one has sufficient strength, but never in two jumps' [62 *p. 4*]. The sparks flew when he met leaders of the Labour Party. By now, Nikita Sergeevich was known as 'the Mouth', and he lived up to his sobriquet. He bragged about the Soviet hydrogen bomb and hinted about a Moscow–Bonn axis. George Brown, a leading Labour politician, browbeat him over political prisoners, whereupon Khrushchev refused to shake his hand. Irate, he spluttered that if this was British socialism, he would prefer to be a Tory.

By the summer of 1956 Khrushchev had evolved his own 'new political thinking' in foreign affairs. Its core was peaceful coexistence. This doctrine dated back to 1952 and resulted from the growing strength of the Soviet Union as a nuclear power. Present policy consisted of improving relations with the great powers; the elimination of sources of conflict which could lead to war; the amelioration of relations with several European states; exploration of ways of solving such problems as European security, disarmament and the German question; *rapprochement* with all countries in the search for peace; expanded contacts with leaders and exchange of delegations. Khrushchev was very optimistic about forming a coalition of the left to join communists in the struggle against war and reaction. He was keen on a Treaty of Friendship and Cooperation with the United States.

DE-STALINISATION AND THE TWENTIETH PARTY CONGRESS

Beria began the process of de-Stalinisation. It was a highly sensitive issue since, if handled badly, it could arouse expectations which could not be realised and thereby provoke unrest. Officials were also ill at ease lest the winds of change cost them their job. Somehow the present leadership had to give the impression that it had not colluded in Stalin's crimes. Releases from labour camps and some rehabilitations provided an appetiser, but a major step was taken in 1955 when the CC set up a commission to investigate Stalin's crimes. Its terms of reference were limited to condemning 'abuses of power' which temporarily blemished an otherwise 'healthy' Party. It was not to condemn Stalin's actions against the 'internal and external enemies of Lenin's party', taken at a time when the new 'socialist party' was being built. This implied that Stalin had been justified in liquidating the Trotskyist and Bukharinist oppositions of the 1920s. Forced industrialisation and collectivisation were also to be defended, despite all the brutalities which accompanied these policies, and so were the purges. Not surprisingly, the commission's report was modest and restricted itself to condemning acts against dedicated Party workers and innocent scientists, writers and other intellectuals [26]. However, within the context of the Soviet Union the report was sensational. The Presidium resolved to engage in a modest attack on Stalin at the upcoming Twentieth Party Congress. Khrushchev seized the initiative and got Presidium permission to redraft the commission's report as part of the CC report, to be delivered by him. This became his famous 'Secret Speech' [*Doc. 11*].

The Congress opened on 14 February 1956. The official reports painted an optimistic picture, with the economy bounding ahead: 1955 was a record agricultural year and 1956 was to be even better. Housing, especially the five-storey blocks without lifts, was booming, and there were more consumer goods and services available. The foreign policy outlook was rosy, especially since the Soviet Union had abandoned Stalin's two-camp theory whereby everyone who was not for the USSR was against it. It was now accepted that there were many roads to socialism. Since there was no specific mention of Stalin in the reports, how was Khrushchev to bring up the list of charges against him? Eventually it was agreed that he should do so, in the name of the CC, at a closed session, after the new CC had been elected. There was to be no discussion of his report. Mikoyan prepared the way for Khrushchev by criticising the master indirectly:

'For twenty years we had no collective leadership: the cult of personality flourished' [77 p. 57]. He announced that some of Stalin's pronouncements had proved erroneous.

The 'Secret Speech' [*Doc. 11*] is a misnomer. It was delivered to Congress delegates and invited guests, but, interestingly, delegates from ruling communist parties and non-communist parties were not invited. They were briefed afterwards, but only in Russian. The revelations contained in the speech ensured that it would become a world-wide sensation (the US Department of State procured a copy from the Poles and published it on 4 June 1956). The report is mainly a violent denunciation of Stalin's many crimes against leading officials and the military between 1934 and 1953. It does not touch on the early years and accepts rapid industrialisation and forced collectivisation as necessary. It is a paean of praise to the Party and a cry of anguish at its suffering. Ordinary mortals are ignored.

There are several reasons for the shortcomings of the 'Secret Speech'. In the first place, it was a compromise and a risky venture. It dared not touch on Stalin's method of rule lest it threatened the position of those who had held high office under and after him. It is a condemnation of Stalin the person and not of the Stalinist system. Even so, Khrushchev's words stunned the delegates. They had worshipped Stalin as a father and infallible leader, but now they were informed that he had originated the purges and tortured victims, including members of the Politburo; that he was responsible for the early defeats of the war; that all the economic ills and failures in foreign policy were his fault; and that he had falsified Party history and his own biography. One delegate was so shocked by the revelations that she was unable to raise her hand to vote acceptance of the report. It was subsequently read out at Party and workplace meetings and met with a hugely positive reaction. So great, in fact, was the reaction that Khrushchev soon had to backtrack. In June 1956 he complimented the master for his 'services' to the Party and the revolutionary movement and toned down Stalin's alleged abuses of power [83]. Khrushchev's retreat put an end to further investigation of Stalin's rule and more denunciations of the crimes he and his agents had perpetrated. Rehabilitating Stalin's victims in the Purge Trials was now off the agenda.

So why did Khrushchev do it? One explanation could be that his purpose was to liberate Party officials from the fear of repression. Under Stalin no one was safe, and the further away from Moscow the better. Nikita Sergeevich felt that if the Party could become an efficient mechanism, stripped of the brutal abuse of power by any individual, it could transform the country and the world. Another possibility is that the demolition of the master was a tactical move in the power struggle at the top of the Party and state. By assaulting Stalin, Khrushchev was undermining the credibility of Molotov, Malenkov, Kaganovich and others who had been members of Stalin's inner circle. They now had a choice: come over to Khrushchev or risk being banished with Stalin. The liberation of millions from the camps after the Congress was a great and good act, indeed a 'miracle', in Solzhenitsyn's view. However, it was due less to political calculation than to a 'movement of the heart' of Khrushchev. He had broken the spell of the Stalin era and was capable of repenting and expiating his crimes.

The Twentieth Party Congress sharpened conflict within the Presidium and the CC. Two new full members were added to the Presidium – Andrei Kirichenko and Mikhail Suslov, both of whom were to play important roles later. No one was dropped. Among the new candidate members were Leonid Brezhnev, Marshal Georgy Zhukov and Dmitry Shepilov, all Khrushchev men. Shepilov was to replace Molotov as foreign minister in June 1956. The composition of the CC changed substantially. Almost half of those elected in 1952 were dropped and fifty-four new names added. Khrushchev's influence here was evident.

The stories which the released prisoners told horrified society. Communists had their Party membership restored and were to be afforded priority in seeking accommodation, work and, if necessary, pensions. Khrushchev was brave enough to admit that he bore some responsibility for Stalin's misdeeds. At a meeting after the Congress he received a note asking him why he had allowed such crimes to be committed. He asked who had written the note. There was total silence. 'The person who wrote this note is frightened. Well, we were frightened to stand up to Stalin' [77 *p. 60*]. At least Nikita Sergeevich was honest.

KHRUSHCHEV AND THE INTELLIGENTSIA

Writers and other intellectuals began demanding greater freedom and the punishment of those who had repressed them. Innovative works appeared, and Ilya Ehrenburg's novel *The Thaw* symbolises the period. There was a remarkable flowering of poetry, and many who later became household names made their appearance at this time, among them Evgeny Evtushenko, Andrei Voznesensky, Okudzhava and Akhmadullina. Evtushenko has described those heady days:

> Literary criticism was lagging hopelessly behind events. Fiction was on the move, but slowly. But poetry was mobile. ... I chose the rostrum as my battleground. I recited poetry in factories, colleges, research institutes, in office buildings and schools. The audiences numbered between twenty and a thousand. In 1963 [poetry readings] attracted 14,000 people to the Sports Palace [122 *p. 101*].

Where else could this have happened? Poetry was the medium of political discourse, and the inflections of the voice were pregnant with meaning. One of the great Russian masters, Osip Mandelshtam, once retorted to his long-suffering wife: 'Why do you complain? Poetry is respected only in this country – people are killed for it' [77 *p. 61*]. This was prophetic. Mandelshtam died in a camp because of a poem which lampooned Stalin.

Khrushchev's relationship with writers and artists was like a piece of barbed wire, smooth in parts but lacerative in others. He lacked the culture and self-confidence to arrive at his own judgements and, hence, was too willing to accept the views of the cultural bureaucrats. However, he knew the Russian classics [*Doc. 18*]. In retirement he confessed he should have read the works which caused such a furore himself, instead of relying on quotations taken out of context. Although he enjoyed the theatre immensely – he went regularly in Moscow in the 1930s and afterwards, whenever he could – he was unwilling to enter into a critical discussion of plays, especially of their artistic merit. His son, Sergei, believed Khrushchev could not free himself from the Bolshevik view that culture was a weapon in the class war. This was a tragedy, since the intelligentsia were strongly on his side in the war against Stalin's legacy.

FOREIGN AFFAIRS AFTER THE CONGRESS

Moscow welcomed many leaders from the Third World after the Congress: Kim Il-Sung from North Korea, Norodom Sihanouk from Cambodia, the Shah of Iran, and Sukarno from Indonesia. Dag Hammarskjöld, the UN Secretary General, also dropped in, as did the French Prime Minister, Guy Mollet, although Khrushchev observed that one did not pay much attention to the composition of French delegations since the government was always changing. This trenchant remark was true at the time, but ceased to be so with the arrival of General Charles de Gaulle and the Fifth Republic.

A Soviet delegation, led by Mikoyan, travelled to Beijing in April 1956 and extended some economic aid to China. In his memoirs Khrushchev scarcely conceals his contempt for China and the Chinese. Mao Zedong returned the favour by visiting Moscow only once under Khrushchev. The experience put him off the Soviet capital for the rest of his life.

If Nikita Sergeevich knew in his bones that relations with the Chinese would not blossom under Mao Zedong, Tito was quite a different proposition. Tito demanded and got the dissolution of the Cominform, which had expelled Yugoslavia in 1948, and changes in the regimes in eastern Europe which were strongly anti-Titoist: Hungary, Romania and Bulgaria. The way was thereby cleared for Tito's first visit to the Soviet Union since 1948. He came in June 1956 and links between the CPSU and the League of Communists of Yugoslavia were resumed.

CRISES IN EASTERN EUROPE

The denunciation of Stalin and the ending of the infallibility of the CPSU were tantamount to lighting a fuse under the east European regimes [*Doc. 5*]. The first conflict occurred in Poland, which had been quiescent when Czechoslovakia and the GDR had flared up after Stalin's death [*Doc. 6i*]. Strikes and street fighting broke out in Poznań on 28 June. The Polish United Workers' Party sided with the workers, calmed their anger and appeared to speak for Polish nationalism. Between July and September the Polish Party took decisions independently of Moscow, and Wladyslaw Gomulka, who had served time and been accused of being a Titoist or national communist, emerged as the leading figure. On 19 October, the CC of the Polish Party convened to elect a new leader, Gomulka. What were the implications of the Polish developments for socialism? Once they had discovered the date of the CC meeting, the Presidium sent Khrushchev, Mikoyan, Molotov and Kaganovich to Warsaw. It was unwilling to allow Nikita Sergeevich to go on his own. Such was the haste that no one informed the Poles, and the Soviet aircraft was intercepted by Polish fighters when crossing the Polish frontier. This was an omen of what was to come. The Poles held their ground and refused to be browbeaten. When Soviet troops were moved up to the Polish frontier, Warsaw made clear it would fight. The Poles demanded, and got, the removal of Marshal Rokossovsky, the Soviet Minister of Defence, in return for a promise to remain close allies of the Soviet Union. The Soviet delegation returned home and left Poland to national communism.

The Polish victory appeared to signal that Moscow welcomed the elimination of Stalinism in eastern Europe. This galvanised the opposition in Hungary, where the Party was disintegrating, the military losing control over its men and the security forces melting away. On 23 October 1956, a huge anti-regime demonstration in Budapest smashed the enormous Stalin statue and vented its spleen on everything Soviet and communist. Soviet troops tried to restore order but in vain. On 28 October, Imre Nagy negotiated a cease-fire and the withdrawal of Soviet troops. On 1 November, he declared that Hungary had left the Warsaw Pact and was now neutral. The Soviets, through their ambassador, Yury Andropov, misled the Hungarian government about their intentions. On 4 November, they sent their troops in to the attack again and, after bitter fighting, took control of the country. Imre Nagy was arrested and later executed. János Kádár was installed as Party leader.

Hungary had presented the divided Soviet leadership with agonising choices, and Khrushchev was blamed by some of his colleagues for fomenting the trouble by denouncing Stalin. Since Hungary was a socialist country, Khrushchev was in the driving seat, but he needed the support of all socialist states to justify military intervention. The Chinese sent Liu Shao-chi to Moscow, whilst Khrushchev and Malenkov flew off to consult the leaders of Poland, Czechoslovakia, Romania and Bulgaria. They then set off for Brioni Island to see Tito. It was a hazardous journey.

> We had to fly through the mountains at night in a fierce thunderstorm. ... During the storm we lost contact with our escort reconnaissance plane which was flying ahead of us. ... The local airfield was poorly equipped. It was one of those primitive airstrips built during the war. ... There was a car waiting for us which took us to a pier. We climbed into a motor launch and headed for Comrade Tito's place on Brioni Island. Malenkov was as pale as a corpse. He gets car sick on a good road. ... He lay down in the boot and shut his eyes. I was worried about what kind of shape he'd be in when we docked, but we didn't have any choice [57 p. 384].

Nikita Sergeevich need not have worried, for he did all the talking. Tito was keen on armed intervention and urged speedy action. This sealed the Hungarians' fate. The Yugoslavs played a further role in the tragedy: Imre Nagy sought political asylum in the Yugoslav embassy in Budapest, but a coach leaving the embassy was stopped and he was arrested. Who gave the order to snatch Nagy? When Nagy was executed two years later Khrushchev was master of the Soviet house and could have intervened but chose not to do so.

Fortunately for the Soviet Union, and unfortunately for Hungary, Britain, France and Israel were preoccupied by their attack on Egypt, following President Nasser's takeover of the Suez Canal. The United States opposed the venture, and Moscow weighed in by threatening to send troops to aid Egypt. The anti-Egyptian coalition backed off and the Soviet Union claimed some of the credit for the Egyptian victory. This whetted Khrushchev's appetite for a greater role in the Middle East. Britain and France being declining powers, Moscow could fill the vacuum. Khrushchev rushed in where wiser counsels would have feared to do so, and despite its military alliance with Egypt and substantial aid, such as the building of the Aswan high dam, the USSR, in the end, reaped few benefits. The Middle East episode would be held against Khrushchev at the CC plenum when he was dismissed in 1964.

NATIONALITY POLICY

Stalin had deported fifty-two nationalities to the east, most after 1944. Khrushchev grasped this nettle at the Twentieth Party Congress and called the policy of removing all the men, women, children, Party and Komsomol members of a particular nation 'monstrous'. However, he rehabilitated only the Kalmyks, Chechens, Ingushi, Karachai and Balkars. He deliberately omitted the two largest deported nations: the Germans and the Crimean Tatars. However, in December 1955 the Germans became the first people to be released from labour camps, to be followed, in April 1956, by the Crimean Tatars, Balkars, Meshkhetians, Khemshins (Muslim Armenians) and Kurds. Tension rose as many deportees headed westward to reclaim their previous homes and property. The Germans had to wait until August 1964 and the Crimean Tatars until September 1967 to be totally rehabilitated and become full citizens again. Khrushchev's nationality policy was not as liberal as Beria's. He wanted Russian to be the medium for the modernisation of the Soviet Union, and was furious when Azerbaijan and Latvia refused to permit parents to choose the language of instruction for their children, for fear that their own language would be swamped by Russian. As a consequence, the Latvian and Azerbaijani Parties and government were purged.

THE FAILED *PUTSCH*

Fortunately for Khrushchev, the harvest was excellent in 1956, because he had provided so many hostages to fortune that a united leadership could have toppled him. He had annoyed Party and state officials by ending supplementary payments which had sometimes come to three times their nominal salary. Moscow had also to pick up the bill for repairs to Hungary, but this meant that less money was available for investment elsewhere. The proposal to decentralise economic decision-making in February 1957 and create *sovnarkhozy* brought opposition to a head, and Nikita Sergeevich's penchant for foreign travel provided his critics with time to plot against him.

Molotov, Malenkov and Kaganovich called a Presidium meeting for 18 June 1957, designed to remove Khrushchev as First Secretary and replace him with Vyacheslav Molotov. If Nikita Sergeevich agreed to go quietly, he would be made Minister of Agriculture. If he resisted, he would be arrested. Molotov and his co-conspirators were confident of a majority in the Presidium. The First Secretary was accused of economic voluntarism – that is, arbitrary and hasty policies – but the main charge against him was that he had gone overboard in condemning Stalin, and had thereby undermined the authority of the CPSU and the international communist movement. Khrushchev vigorously defended himself, but was supported by only Mikoyan, Suslov and Kirichenko among the full Presidium members. Seven Presidium members, including Molotov, Malenkov, Voroshilov, Kaganovich and Bulganin, opposed him. Five candidate members, headed by Zhukov and Brezhnev, sided with him, but as candidate members they could speak but not vote. Brezhnev's speech was very crudely interrupted by Kaganovich, and he was so shocked that he almost fainted. One candidate member, Zhukov, made quite an impact by stressing that the military supported him and would not move without his (Zhukov's) order. Shepilov began by supporting Khrushchev, then changed sides.

Khrushchev argued that the Presidium could not sack him; only the CC could do that. He demanded that it be convened, but Molotov and Malenkov refused. However, pro-Khrushchev CC members were summoned to Moscow and gradually the pressure to convene proved irresistible. The CC plenum met in Moscow from 22 to 29 June, and it was a foregone conclusion that Khrushchev would carry the day. Only Molotov had the guts to oppose Nikita Sergeevich in the CC and he abstained from the resolution confirming Khrushchev in office. The others backed down and made penitent speeches.

The decree of the plenum was published only on 4 July 1957, and much was made of the Anti-Party group, consisting of Malenkov, Molotov, Kaganovich and Shepilov, 'who had joined them'. The opposition of Bulganin, Voroshilov and the others was passed over in silence. The Presidium was now enlarged to fifteen members, and among the new full members were Leonid Brezhnev, Frol Kozlov and Marshal Georgy Zhukov. Among the new candidate members were Aleksei Kosygin and Andrei Kirilenko. Andrei Gromyko replaced Shepilov as foreign minister. At least one of the losers feared for his life. Two days after the plenum Kaganovich phoned Khrushchev: 'Comrade Khrushchev, I have known you for many years. I beg you not to allow them to deal with me as they dealt with people under Stalin.' Khrushchev replied: 'Comrade Kaganovich, your words confirm once again what methods you wanted to use to attain your vile ends. You wanted the country to revert to the order that existed under the personality cult. You wanted to kill people. You measure others by your own yardstick. But you are mistaken. We apply Leninist principles with vigour and will continue to apply them. You will be given a job. You will be able to work and live in peace if you work honestly like all Soviet people' [121 p. 588].

None of Khrushchev's opponents was expelled from the Party, but all were given tasks away from Moscow; for example, Molotov became ambassador to Mongolia. Bulganin stayed on as Prime Minister until the following year and Voroshilov remained head of state until 1960. In fact, however, Khrushchev was now on top of the tree, head of the Party and government. The new Presidium mirrored this shift. Hitherto those holding government office had been in the majority, but now those in Party posts dominated. The Party apparatus had taken over and this remained in charge until Gorbachev became executive President in 1989.

SPUTNIK

On 4 October 1957, the Soviet Union amazed and stunned the world by launching the first artificial Earth satellite. Sputnik revealed the great strides taken by the Soviets in missile technology and the potential to built intercontinental ballistic missiles (ICBM). A month later, another satellite was launched, with a dog on board. The Americans began a feverish review of their missile technology but were not able to get a satellite into space until February 1958. Sputnik was a marvellous present for the fortieth anniversary of the October Revolution, which was celebrated with great élan on 7 November 1957 and attended by representatives from almost all Communist Parties. Two conferences were held to drive home the message of de-Stalinisation: one of the twelve ruling parties, and the other in which sixty-four communist and workers' parties participated.

Mao, a peacock of a man, felt that, as the natural successor to Stalin in the world communist movement, he should be consulted about Soviet developments [*Doc. 8ii*]. Mao and Khrushchev disagreed on most points, especially on nuclear weapons [*Doc. 8i*]. Mao saw the Americans as 'paper tigers' but Khrushchev knew they were real tigers. Marshal Zhukov had proved too independent as Minister of Defence. For instance, in the summer of 1957 he introduced military reforms without consulting the Party, and he treated political officers in the military with contempt. Zhukov had to be got rid of because he posed a threat to the Party's dominance.

3 ON TOP OF THE WORLD, 1958–62

After Khrushchev had pushed Bulganin aside in March 1958 and become Prime Minister, a Defence Council was established. Naturally Khrushchev became the commander-in-chief of Soviet armed forces. All the glittering prizes offered by the Party and the state were his. It was enough to turn anyone's head. However, formulating policy is one thing but implementing it is another. Khrushchev had great authority. He was the chief decision-maker and had become a strong, national leader, but since he was not willing to use coercion he needed to convince officials, workers and the rest of the population that his policies were good for them. In other words, he needed legitimacy. Lower-level officials would grant him this, as would most of the population, but top officials were opposed to any decentralisation of decision-making as this would undermine their power and patronage. Khrushchev needed the support of the top officials, because collectively they could topple him. His reforms were bound to alienate some group. It was up to him not to allow all the aggrieved groups to come together and form a coalition against him.

Nikita Sergeevich had great political gifts, but he lacked a team to tackle the economic and other problems bequeathed by the Stalin era. Ideally, he needed a talented supporter who had extensive experience of industry and agriculture and who could coordinate and implement economic policy. Aleksei Kosygin might have performed this role admirably and acted as a restraining influence on Nikita Sergeevich's brilliant but erratic ideas. Apparently, Khrushchev did propose Kosygin as Prime Minister in 1958, but the general opinion in the Presidium was that Khrushchev should take over. He was at his reforming peak between 1958 and 1962, able to force through any piece of legislation, but it must be admitted that much of it was ill conceived, ill digested and doomed to fail before the ink was dry on the documents. There was no overall plan, no strategy of reform. It usually began with Nikita Sergeevich having a wizard idea, and so enthusiastic would he become that he would brush aside all objections. Khrushchev was brilliant at lateral thinking – providing several solutions to the same problem – but as time passed the number of options declined and he often chose the wrong one. He would dictate his inspirational thoughts, then read the transcript, make amendments and finally hand it over for drafting as legislation. Often the drafters were not clear what the ultimate objective was, as becomes painfully clear when one rereads the legislation. There were formidable institutional barriers to radical change in the Soviet Union – Gorbachev can testify to that – but it is clear that the personal factor played an important role. Khrushchev believed passionately that he had a mission to transform the Soviet Union into a land of plenty in which justice and democracy would reign. As an evangelist he was as full of eloquence as he was empty of doubt about the ultimate communist goal. Unfortunately for him, the number of agnostics increased steadily, so that by 1964 there were practically no believers left. Nikita Sergeevich personally must shoulder much of the blame for this débâcle.

EDUCATION

Khrushchev was shocked to discover how dominant the intelligentsia had become among students in higher education. One reason for this was that under legislation introduced by Stalin, fees had to be paid for higher education and the upper forms of secondary education. This excluded all but the very gifted from the working class and the collective farm peasantry: one of these was Gorbachev, but he was at Moscow State University mainly due to Party patronage. There was also a need to improve the training of young people for industry.

In July 1958, therefore, Khrushchev launched an educational reform programme which attacked the elitism of the intelligentsia and top Party and government officials, particularly their aversion, and that of their children, to manual labour. Khrushchev called for a re-emphasis on vocational training and the raising of the prestige of manual jobs in industry and agriculture. Training in production was to take up one-third of school time in the final three years and pupils were to spend several months working in actual factories. He also eased the passage of working-class pupils to university and higher education. Evening and correspondence courses expanded rapidly. Primary education was to be extended from seven to eight years, but the overall period of schooling was reduced from eleven to ten years.

The reform was unpopular for various reasons. Factories objected to having schoolchildren cluttering up their premises, since they had enough to do without having to train them. Intelligentsia parents were appalled at the prospect of their children working in factories and failing to gain a coveted place at university, a passport to an intelligentsia job. Heads of higher educational establishments saw the reform as lowering academic standards. Opposition was so strong that these changes were reversed when Khrushchev was removed in 1964.

REFORMING THE KGB

The time had come to reform the KGB. It was replete with officers – beginning with General Ivan Serov, the head – whose pasts were murky, to put it mildly. Roy Medvedev thinks that the scandal of the Queen of the Belgians' crown provided an ideal pretext [81]. The Germans had looted the crown during the war and it had subsequently disappeared. After a long investigation it turned up in Serov's very extensive private collection. He was as avid a magpie as Marshal Hermann Goering, and had bagged it while working for *Smersh* (Soviet counter-intelligence) in Germany. The crown was returned to Belgium, but Serov was too useful to Khrushchev to be disgraced. Instead, he was made head of the GRU or military intelligence, whose activities were beyond public scrutiny.

Khrushchev settled on Aleksandr Shelepin, first secretary of the Komsomol or Young Communist League, as the new chief of the KGB. Shelepin was young, dynamic and ferociously ambitious. He turned the KGB upside down and brought in a large number of Komsomol officials. This promised to make the security police a Party tool. Later, Khrushchev saw Shelepin as a possible successor, but perceived that his lack of industrial experience was a weakness. He proposed to him that he move to Leningrad and become first Party secretary there. Shelepin saw this as a demotion and refused. They thereupon fell out, and Shelepin was one of those who engineered Khrushchev's removal in 1964.

CULTURE

Talented writers were impatient to publish what they had been writing in private but kept in the 'bottom drawer', as the saying goes. V. Dudintsev published *Not by Bread Alone* in 1956. The novel is about a scientist who has to fight the establishment –

scholars, managers and Party officials. The journal *Novy Mir*, under its chief editors Konstantin Simonov and Aleksandr Tvardovsky, became one of the focal points of the new era.

Boris Pasternak offered his 'bottom drawer' novel, *Dr Zhivago*, (this means 'living' in pre–1918 orthography) to *Novy Mir* but was turned down. The journal supported democratic socialism and hence was not willing to publicise Pasternak's rejection of the October revolution. The work eventually ended up in the hands of Feltrinelli, a left-wing Italian publisher who brought it out in 1957. The following year it was awarded the Nobel Prize. The establishment descended on Pasternak like a pack of wolves. *Literaturnaya Gazeta* called him a 'literary Judas who has betrayed his people for thirty pieces of silver, the Nobel Prize' [77 *p. 79*]. Vladimir Semichastny, first secretary of the Komsomol, was more earthy at a plenum of the Komsomol Central Committee, describing Pasternak as a 'pig who had fouled his own sty' [77 *p. 79*]. One doctor claimed that the novel was a disgrace to the medical profession, which is an interesting observation given that it was not available in the Soviet Union. A terrible joke circulated in the capital: 'Moscow is suffering from three plagues: *rak* (cancer), Spartak (a Moscow football team doing badly) and Pasternak' [77 *p. 80*]. Pasternak declined the Nobel Prize, but the furore shortened his life. When he died in May 1960, his funeral brought together a latent independent intelligentsia, whose presence was a protest against the oppressive nature of the regime. The whole disgraceful episode lost the Soviet Union face abroad, and in retirement, after having read the novel, Khrushchev came to regret the whole affair [*Doc. 9*].

THE MILITARY

Another group with whom Khrushchev was frequently crossing swords was the military. The defence budget was pared in 1953 and 1954, and Khrushchev was hungry for more. By 1958 the military had lost 2 million men. Nikita Sergeevich had begun to see missiles as the weapons of the future. He had clashed with Zhukov, a solidly ground-forces' man, over this. In December 1959, the Strategic Rocket Forces were established as a separate service responsible for regional and intercontinental missiles. This service was to be pre-eminent in wartime, replacing ground-forces. In a speech to the USSR Supreme Soviet in January 1960 Khrushchev emphasised the primary importance of nuclear weapons and missiles. As a consequence, he said, many of the traditional armed forces were becoming obsolete. Manpower was therefore to be reduced from 3.6 million to 2.4 million, but the vacuum left by this reduction would be more than filled by nuclear fire-power. In late 1959 Khrushchev and Marshal Malinovsky made statements which implied that the Soviets were going ahead with their ICBM building programme and claimed nuclear parity with the United States. In early 1960 Khrushchev stated that any country which dared attack the Soviet Union would be wiped off the map with missiles carrying atomic and thermonuclear warheads, but in fact this capacity did not exist. By 1960 the USSR had deployed only four ICBMs and 145 heavy bombers of intercontinental range, but Khrushchev boasted that the Soviet Union could hit a fly in space and the Americans began to perceive a 'missile gap' (which in reality was non-existent) and set about eliminating it.

The reasons behind Khrushchev's high-risk strategy appear to have been his exaggerated belief in missiles, the looming labour shortage due to the sharp fall in the birth rate during the war and the need to save money. Nuclear forces are cheaper than conventional (non-nuclear) forces the world over. Khrushchev was updating Soviet military doctrine, but many top officers disagreed with his premises. The military had another gripe. No preparations had been made to ease the transition of the demobbed officers and men into civilian life.

THE POLICE

Krushchev then turned his attention to the police. He proposed the abolition of the all-union (USSR) Ministry of Internal Affairs (MVD) and the devolution of its duties to republican Ministries for the Safeguarding of Public Order (MOOP). The civil police, the militia and the MOOP officers were also to lose some of their privileges, which, according to Khrushchev, had become excessive under Stalin. Nikita Sergeevich was making himself unpopular with the guardians of national and domestic security. Neither did he endear himself to those working in Siberia and the Soviet Far East. After visiting the regions he came to the conclusion that the many bonuses and benefits paid to workers there should be abolished. This speeded up migration from the north and east to the more hospitable regions of European Russia and the south – a policy which had later to be reversed in order to attract labour to the new industries, especially oil and gas.

CHANGES IN THE LEADERSHIP

There was a leadership reshuffle in May 1960. A CC plenum promoted Aleksei Kosygin, Nikolai Podgorny and Dmitry Polyansky to full membership of the Presidium. Those going down included Andrei Kirichenko, who was sacked from the Presidium and Secretariat. He had been close to Nikita Sergeevich and had chaired meetings of the Presidium and Secretariat when the First Secretary was away on some of his jaunts. He may have been blamed for the agricultural failures of 1959. He was replaced as a CC secretary by Frol Kozlov. Kozlov was regarded as a conservative, but Khrushchev ignored this.

Another comrade to be removed from the Presidium was Nikolai Belyaev, first Party secretary in Kazakhstan, who had promised more than he could deliver in that prime virgin lands region. His successor was the Kazakh Dinmukhamed Kunaev, who was to remain in office until sacked by Gorbachev in 1986. Voroshilov was at long last removed as head of state and replaced by Leonid Brezhnev. (This demonstrated that the role of Soviet head of state was not regarded as politically significant. It remained so until Podgorny.)

SOCIAL POLICY

One measure which pleased many was the abolition of income tax and the tax on bachelors and spinsters earning less than 500 roubles a month. A seven-hour working day was gradually to be phased in.

Another monetary reform was not as welcome. As of 1 January 1961 ten old roubles were to be worth one new rouble. People simply did not believe that the rouble in their pocket had retained its value. Psychologically, a large bundle of notes appears to confer a nice warm feeling. This is one of the reasons why Italians earn millions of lire a month. The suspicions of the Soviet population were well founded. State prices stayed firm but the private market saw the change as a heaven-sent opportunity to make some extra money.

FOREIGN POLICY

Yugoslavia

Khrushchev's courtship of Tito did not bear much fruit. Indeed, the Yugoslav communists went their own way, and their draft programme, published in the summer of 1958, was judged 'revisionist' by CPSU ideologues. This was a very insulting term and raised the hackles of Belgrade. Khrushchev went further and referred to Yugoslavia as a Trojan horse in the world communist movement. He also postponed credits which were to begin in 1958 and stopped the shipment of wheat which had already been agreed. In both cases he broke contractual agreements, but that was his style.

China, 1958

Relations with China also deteriorated in 1958. Mao regarded a third world war as inevitable and accused Khrushchev of being too soft on the imperialists. China's 'Great Leap Forward' to communism was under way, accompanied by ever-increasing demands for aid from the Soviet Union and eastern Europe. When he was in Beijing, Khrushchev declined to commit the Soviet Union to side militarily with China in its conflict with Taiwan and the United States. The Chinese also asked for Soviet help in developing a nuclear capacity. Mao understood Khrushchev to have agreed, but Moscow always denied this.

The Lebanon

During the summer of 1958 the United States invaded Lebanon. The Arab states felt threatened and called for Soviet support. Nasser visited Moscow to underline the message, and eventually the Americans withdrew their troops. It was quite a diplomatic victory for Nikita Sergeevich.

Albania

Khrushchev liked to visit eastern Europe, where he played the *grand seigneur*. However, in May 1959 he went to Albania and did not get on at all with Enver Hoxha and the leadership, which was Stalinist and preferred to stay so. Some of Hoxha's opponents within the Albanian Party travelled to Moscow to lobby Khrushchev's support, but this only prompted Hoxha to order the shooting of three top officials, one of them a pregnant woman. Khrushchev also records that another Albanian woman official was strangled because, on a stopover in Moscow, *en route* from Beijing to Tirana, she had briefed the Soviets on the discussions with the Chinese. It came as no surprise when Albania broke with the Soviet Union in 1961, and also left the Warsaw Pact and Comecon, the socialist trade organisation. Albania thereafter became a fierce critic of the Soviet Union, often in tandem with China, and Nikita Sergeevich was a special target for their venom.

Berlin

After accepting the reality of two German states in 1958 the Soviets were left with the problem of Berlin, which was under four-power control. Ulbricht explained to Khrushchev that socialism could not be built successfully in the GDR as long as the frontier between East and West Berlin remained open. Moscow therefore began in November 1958 to attempt to squeeze Britain, the United States and France out of West Berlin, intending to transform it into a 'free city'. If the West did not agree by May 1959, the Soviet Union would conclude a treaty with the GDR handing over its rights to East Berlin. The West would then have to negotiate rights of access to West Berlin with the GDR, which, as a member of the Warsaw Pact, could call on the assistance of that organisation if a dispute arose. The West, however, stood firm and proposed a foreign ministers' conference in Geneva, whereupon Moscow withdrew its ultimatum. The Berlin crisis lasted about four years. Its tensest moment was in August 1961, when Khrushchev finally conceded that the Allies could not be forced out of West Berlin. Instead the Berlin Wall was built [*Docs 15, 18*].

The United States

The US exhibition in Sokolniki Park in Moscow provided the context for a famous exchange between Nikita Sergeevich and Vice-President Richard Nixon. While touring the exhibition Khrushchev was irritated by Nixon's air of effortless superiority. Ending up in the kitchen of the model American home, Nikita Sergeevich delivered himself of an earthy saying. His message was that if the Americans wanted to have a go, the Soviets would teach them a lesson. However, the US interpreter was flummoxed by the expression and translated it literally: 'We'll show you Kuzma's mother.' This gave rise to great hilarity afterwards, as the expression is used as a euphemism for a sensitive part of the male anatomy. Khrushchev was longing to visit the United States. He received an invitation to go there in September 1959, to 'get to know the country and the people'. The visit would be the first by the head of the Soviet government or Party. His entourage included Nina Petrovna, his wife, and other members of the family. Nikita Sergeevich could hardly get over being invited:

Who would have guessed, twenty years ago, that the most powerful capitalist country would invite a communist to visit? This is incredible. Today they *have* to take us into account. It's our strength that led to this – they have to recognize our existence and our power. Who would have thought the capitalists would invite me, a worker? Look what we've achieved in these years [62 *p. 356*].

One does not need to be a psychologist to diagnose that Nikita Sergeevich was suffering from an inferiority complex.

Uncle Sam loved him. His dynamism, openness, earthiness, love of good drink, vitality and sheer *joie de vivre* went down a treat. An American look-alike made a good living afterwards impersonating Nikita Sergeevich. Khrushchev gave as good as he got. Upbraided by the Washington press on human rights and other sensitive issues, he exclaimed: 'If you throw dead rats at me, I'll throw dead rats at you!' [81 *p. 148*]. In Washington he met John F. Kennedy for the first time. In New York he addressed the United Nations and stressed the need for peaceful coexistence, disarmament and the avoidance of nuclear war – the main themes of his visit. In Los Angeles he was riled by the mayor's speech, which was acerbic and wounding. Nikita Sergeevich then performed his famous exploding act, making it clear that he represented a great power and would not be treated in such a manner. He even enquired if his plane was ready, for Vladivostok was not far away. The lugubrious Andrei Gromyko was dispatched to convey a similar message to Henry Cabot Lodge, who was accompanying the Soviet delegation around the country. Khrushchev's tactics were successful, for the next day, in San Francisco, all was sweetness and light. He later said that his visit had broken the ice. It was now up to the diplomats to remove the lumps. Khrushchev picked up a few useful tips as well. Self-service restaurants were a revelation and were promptly adopted in the Soviet Union. Khrushchev also discovered that many Americans travelled by train at night in sleeping compartments, and this too was taken up at home in a big way. The US visit was accompanied by enormous publicity in the Soviet Union and left an indelible impression on Khrushchev and the Soviet people.

China, 1959, and the Far East

The day after he returned from America, Khrushchev repaired to Beijing, but he got a frosty reception. Hobnobbing with the imperialists was not what a Soviet leader should be doing, in the eyes of the Chinese. He had only a brief meeting with Mao, who explained that he was too busy. Tension was increasing between the Soviet and east European advisers and their Chinese hosts, bent as they were on implementing the 'Great Leap Forward'. This was causing economic damage, and the advisers were right in calling it the 'Great Leap Backward'. Khrushchev left quickly, soon to be followed by the specialists, and they took the blueprints of their plans with them. This particularly riled the Chinese, who vowed never again to become dependent on an outside power. The rift was probably inevitable, but Nikita Sergeevich's undiplomatic and insensitive behaviour hastened it. In early 1960 he was off to India again, then to Burma and Indonesia. Various agreements on economic and cultural cooperation were signed and students were invited to study in the Soviet Union, but they were not popular since they were afforded preferential treatment. Homeward bound he dropped in on the Afghans.

The West and the U2 Crisis

Then he was off to France, where the communists were strong but up against General de Gaulle, who was attempting to consolidate the young Fifth Republic. Khrushchev was introduced to vintage champagne and he underestimated its potency. He ended up doing the *gopak*, a traditional dance, which involves a lot of jumping and bending and is best left to the young. Later he asked de Gaulle if his foreign minister would do anything he asked. The response was positive. Thereupon Nikita Sergeevich asserted that his own foreign minister, Andrei Andreevich Gromyko, would do anything for him. If ordered, he would even drop his trousers and sit on a block of ice.

The superpowers agreed on a summit meeting in Paris, beginning on 16 May 1960. However, an American U2 reconnaissance aircraft was shot down by a missile over Sverdlovsk (Ekaterinburg) on 1 May 1960. When Khrushchev reported this he did not give the location. The pilot, Gary Powers, was under orders to destroy his aircraft and not provide any information. The United States talked about a plane investigating meteorological conditions over Turkey and Iran having strayed into Soviet air space, but Khrushchev countered this by revealing the location and also that the pilot had survived and was giving information to the Soviets. When he arrived in Paris, Khrushchev demanded that President Eisenhower condemn and cease all such overflights, punish those involved and apologise. The US President refused and thereupon had his invitation to visit the USSR withdrawn. The two countries now reverted to hurling abuse at one another.

Khrushchev at the UN

Meanwhile, the revolution in Cuba in 1959, led by Fidel Castro, was becoming increasingly anti-American. This made a *rapprochement* with Moscow a natural development. The United States had imposed a trade embargo and left Castro no option but to develop relations with the socialist world if he was to survive. Khrushchev decided to attend the UN General Assembly in September 1960, sailing in the *Baltika* along with the Party leaders of Hungary, Romania and Bulgaria. When the *Baltika* arrived in New York, however, it docked not at a grand pier but at a miserable, dilapidated one, for the Soviets were strapped for hard currency and had to save money. Hence they ended up among the poor relations.

Khrushchev visited Castro's modest hotel in Harlem for their first meeting. He also met Tito. His speech at the UN claimed world headlines, but his behaviour was deliberately disruptive. He interrupted speakers from the floor, disparagingly dismissing the Philippines delegate as a 'lackey of American imperialism'. He rowed with Secretary General Dag Hammarskjöld over UN behaviour in the Congo; he proposed that a 'troika' be set up to replace him, on the grounds that Hammarskjöld was 'hopelessly biased'; and he banged his shoe on his desk to underline his displeasure. (Harold Macmillan, the British Prime Minister, responded by calmly asking for a translation!) The UN was not pleased and fined the Soviet delegation US$10,000 for bad behaviour. Embarrassed Soviet diplomats attempted to present 'shoe' diplomacy as something novel – which it was – and intended to underline Khrushchev's determination to fight imperialism. In fact, it was nothing of the kind. It was mere showmanship, which presented the Soviet leader in a poor light. Such undisciplined behaviour suggested that the man in control of the Kremlin was not in control of himself.

However, it may all have been an act. With the Soviets needing to cut defence spending, switch resources to the civil economy and overcome the shortage of labour resulting from the fall in the birth rate, Khrushchev may have thought that the best way to scare off the Americans was to threaten them with his non-existent missile arsenal. His unpredictable demeanour would warn the West that it was far too risky to put pressure on him. If this was his rationale he was way off line. Instead of slowing down the arms race he accelerated it, for the Americans took him and his threats at face value.

Tension between Moscow and Beijing

Increasing Chinese anger at the policies of the Soviet Union was not mere acting but the real thing. Border clashes between China and India, in early 1960, added fuel to the fire. The Chinese took it for granted that Moscow would support them, but the Soviets were cultivating India and merely published both sides of the dispute. Soviet invitations to the Chinese government and Mao to visit Moscow went unanswered. The two communist giants were no longer on speaking terms. On the ninetieth anniversary of Lenin's birth, in April 1960, the Chinese published a lengthy analysis of Leninism and claimed that they, rather than the Soviets, were the true standard-bearers of Leninist revolutionary tradition. At the Romanian Communist Party Congress, in June 1960, the Soviets and the Chinese fought for supremacy in front of the embarrassed delegates.

An international conference of communist and workers' parties convened in Moscow in November 1960. Eighty-one parties attended, but not the Yugoslavs. It was a watershed. About a dozen parties sided with the Chinese on Soviet home ground. Moscow was no longer the leader of the world communist movement. There were now two camps, with the Yugoslavs outside. Under Lenin and Stalin communism was monocentric – Moscow rule prevailed – but it had now become polycentric. There were now many roads to communism. Khrushchev's determination to pursue de-Stalinisation had split the Soviet Union. Now it had split the world movement.

THE TWENTY-FIRST PARTY CONGRESS

With the Chinese at his heels, Nikita Sergeevich had to demonstrate that his economic policies were brilliantly successful. The harvest in 1957 had not come up to expectations – the tradition under Khrushchev was that even years were good and odd years bad. It was becoming clear that the Five Year Plan 1956–60 would not be achieved. Nikita Sergeevich had a brainwave. If five years were not long enough to succeed, why not introduce a seven year plan? The best forum to launch such an initiative was a Party Congress, but the next one was only due in 1960. So he called an Extraordinary Congress, the Twenty-First, in January 1959.

It launched a very ambitious economic plan with industrial output to rise by 80 per cent by 1965. There was to be a chemical revolution; production was to grow by 300 per cent. Emphasis was to be concentrated on modern technologies, especially those pioneered by successes in space. Living standards were to rise sharply with many more consumer goods becoming available. Fifteen million flats were to be constructed and another 7 million dwellings in the countryside.

The relentless pressure to increase agricultural output began to take its toll. Ryazan *oblast* promised to increase greatly its meat deliveries to the state in 1959, but how could this be done? One way was to decimate animal numbers, but this would have a disastrous impact on meat production in 1960 and thereafter. Someone hit on a solution. Buy from the peasants. But this would only cover part of the total. Why not rustle cattle in other *oblasts*? This could only be done at night, so nocturnal expeditions took off in all directions to steal every animal to be found. Rustling animals meant that other *oblasts* would not fulfil their plan, but that was their problem. Even so, there was a shortfall, so another wheeze was tried: buy the animals from the peasants, record them as state deliveries, sell them back to the peasants, then buy them back again, until the plan had been fulfilled – at least on paper! Sooner or later the balloon was bound to go up. When it did, the first Party secretary went the way of his animals. He shot himself. Khrushchev railed about the padding of production statistics, but he should have known better. The penalty for failure was so high that 'success' had to be reported.

ECONOMIC PROBLEMS

Khrushchev was aware that a key reason for the unsatisfactory performance of the rural sector was lack of investment. There was a sharp fall in investment in 1958 with the rate of growth of investment falling from 12.8 per cent in 1958 to 7 per cent in 1959 and 2.4 per cent in 1960. During the years 1958–64 annual deliveries of trucks, grain combines, cultivators, seeders and maize silage harvesters dropped below the levels of 1956–57. The result was that the share of agriculture in total investment fell from 17.6 per cent in 1956 to 14.2 per cent in 1960, but rose to 17.4 per cent in 1964.

Denied more resources for agriculture, Khrushchev tried to compensate by launching campaigns to change cropping patterns in order to boost production. He campaigned for the extension of maize as a fodder crop and it replaced more suitable crops in many areas. Between 1953 and 1963 the area under rye was cut back by a quarter and oats by almost two-thirds. Maize replaced winter wheat in Ukraine and north Caucasus. However, lack of suitable machinery caused delays and resulted in poor crops. Khrushchev also thought that too much land was under grass and clean fallow, so between 1960 and 1963 the grass area was reduced by a half and clean fallow by almost two-thirds. This was forced on north Kazakhstan, where it was opposed by A. Baraev, a leading agronomist, but Nikita Sergeevich would not listen. The result was weed infestation and erosion.

In 1963 an early spring thaw and drought led to the soil drying out in the virgin lands. The harvest failure was almost total and millions of tonnes of topsoil were blown away. Khrushchev lost his battle for a shift of resources into agriculture. The heavy industry and defence lobbies were too powerful for him. Thus his braggadocio in foreign and security affairs reduced the amount of resources flowing into the agrarian sector. However, there were some successes to record. Grain and animal husbandry output over the years 1961–64 was significantly higher than in 1957–60, but unfortunately far short of public expectations. By 1965 the actual increase was only 20 per cent of the planned increase set in 1958.

In order to motivate peasants to put in more work on kolkhozes and sovkhozes Khrushchev 'encouraged' them to sell their livestock to the farms. But this made them less self-sufficient, and as they turned to state shops to make up the shortfall the state retail network came under increasing pressure. In March 1962, Khrushchev proposed a revamping of agricultural administration. An All-Union Committee for Agriculture was set up, supervised by a hierarchy of Party-dominated agricultural committees. Almost 1,000 Territorial Production Administrations (TPA) were established. Each TPA was assigned a Party organiser, who acted as the obkom's agent in ensuring that farms fulfilled their plans. (Gorbachev became a Party organiser in Stavropol *krai*.) The official appointed to chair the All-Union Committee, N. G. Ignatev, demoted from the Party Presidium, was later to play an important role in coordinating opposition to Khrushchev in 1964. He was typical of many who felt let down by Khrushchev.

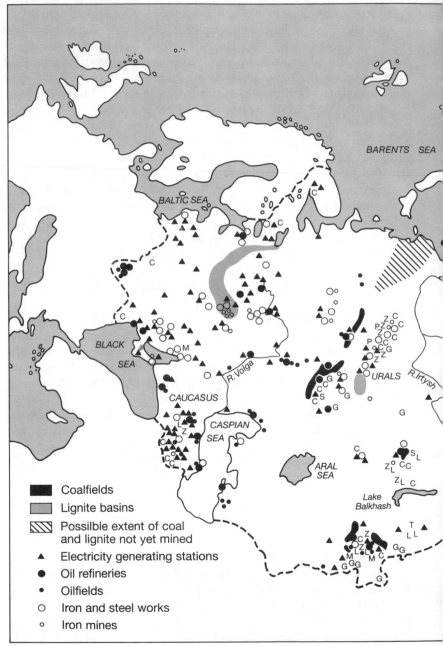

Map 2 Soviet heavy industry and its raw materials (After: Martin Gilbert, *The Russian History Atlas*, Routledge, London.)

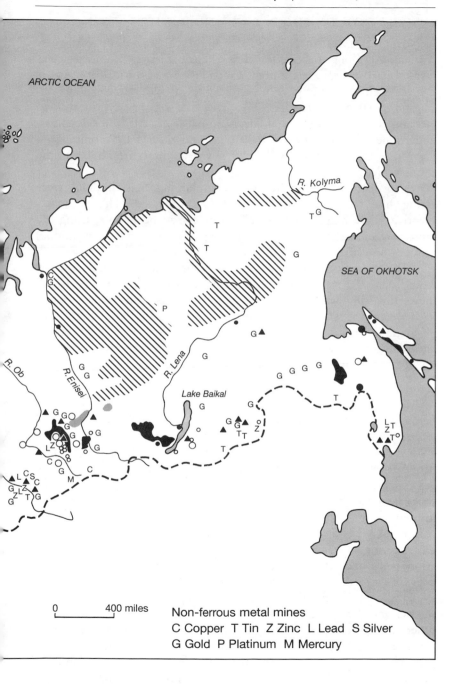

ARCTIC OCEAN

R. Kolyma

SEA OF OKHOTSK

R. Ob

R. Enisei

R. Lena

Lake Baikal

0   400 miles

Non-ferrous metal mines
C Copper T Tin Z Zinc L Lead S Silver
G Gold P Platinum M Mercury

BIFURCATION OF THE PARTY AND SOVIETS

In November 1962, the whole Party and local soviet apparatus was reorganised along production lines. Each *oblast* committee was divided into separate committees for industry and agriculture. At the lowest level, the *raion* gave way to 'zones of industrial production' and, in rural areas, to the TPA. The goal of the reform was to increase control over local decision-making. All these changes undermined the authority of the *oblast* and *raion* Party committees. Previously they, together with their soviet counterparts, had run the countryside.

By April 1964 Khrushchev was complaining that the TPA were acting like the organisations they had replaced. This was not surprising, given that they were run by the same people, using the same work methods. The bewildering number of organisational changes sowed confusion and promoted failure. Nikita Sergeevich was always seeking for the piece of string, which, when pulled, would set the Soviet economic mechanism working perfectly. Inevitably, this was a fruitless search. Farms and farm workers needed to be stimulated through adjustments to the price mechanism. Even by 1964 animal husbandry was loss-making almost everywhere. This meant that the more that was produced, the greater the loss to the farm.

Food Problems

In an attempt to recoup from the population some of the cost of higher procurement prices the retail price of butter was increased by 25 per cent and that of meat by 30 per cent on 1 June 1962. Sugar dropped by 5 per cent but this did not assuage the sense of grievance felt by consumers. In Novocherkassk workers went on strike against the increases. Troops fired on them and killed and injured many.

Khrushchev changed almost all the Ministers of Agriculture at the centre and in the republics, and replaced them with men who had a good track record as sovkhoz managers. However, 1963 was a disastrous year. A crash programme was launched to increase the availability of chemical fertilisers and herbicides, but they were of limited value in dry farming areas due to the lack of moisture. The other innovation was to import millions of tonnes of grain from Canada, Australia and other countries, for cash. The events of Novocherkassk may have influenced this decision. It was a laudable one, nevertheless. Stalin would have let the population starve.

SUCCESSES IN SPACE

If the Soviet Union could not solve the food problem, it was quite a different story in space. The impact of Sputnik was dwarfed by the first manned space flight on 12 April 1961. Yury Gagarin became a hero at home and abroad. The Americans were left behind and President Kennedy announced the Apollo mission to put an American on the moon. The in-joke was that when he landed he would be met by a short, fat man who would explain to him how to grow maize there.

THE CUBAN MISSILE CRISIS

President John F. Kennedy inherited a plan to invade Cuba and drive Castro out, but the CIA and Cuban émigrés got everything wrong and the Bay of Pigs invasion was routed, with Castro leading his troops personally. He needed help to repel another possible invasion, and soon Soviet military advisers arrived. Kennedy decided he would like to meet Khrushchev on neutral ground before agreeing to a possible summit. The meeting took place in Vienna on 3–4 June 1961, but there was no agenda and no communiqué. Nikita Sergeevich was feeling on top of the world after Soviet achievements in space and the Bay of Pigs fiasco. Kennedy remarked that he found the meeting 'sobering' and expected a 'cold winter'. On 15 June Khrushchev again threatened to sign a peace treaty with the GDR if the West refused an all-German treaty. When the Americans announced an increase in the defence budget, Khrushchev retorted angrily that he was thinking of resuming atomic testing and exploding a 100-megatonne bomb. This alarmed many people, including Academician Andrei Sakharov [*Doc. 16*]. In fact, Khrushchev eventually climbed down and instead supported the building of the Berlin Wall, designed, in his own words, to 'guard the gates of the socialist paradise'. By doing so, Khrushchev was acknowledging something about which the average Soviet citizen was absolutely unaware – namely, that 'the GDR, and not only the GDR – has yet to reach a level of moral and material development where competition with the West is possible' [57 p. 419].

At the Twenty-second Party Congress, in October 1961, Marshal Rodion Malinovsky, the Minister of Defence, reiterated Soviet claims to military superiority. However, by now the United States had perceived there was no missile gap and was engaged in a strategic build-up which promised to give the Americans a lead in long-distance missiles. Khrushchev was haunted by the thought that the Americans would have another go at Castro [*Doc. 17*]. On 30 November 1961 President Kennedy authorised Operation Mongoose, to 'help Cuba overthrow the communist regime'. The Cubans penetrated the CIA, and obtained a document which stated that if Castro had not gone by October 1962 tougher measures would have to be taken. In late September and October 1962 Robert McNamara, Secretary for Defence, authorised active preparations for an invasion of Cuba. The Cubans understood 'tougher measures' to mean invasion and passed the material on to the KGB and thence to Khrushchev. The Soviet leader immediately informed his colleagues that America was going to invade Cuba and that he had to do something. McNamara ordered the intensification of planning and preparations for action to the 'highest state of readiness' to ensure that an invasion of Cuba would be possible by 20 October.

Khrushchev proposed to place missiles on Cuba, much to the delight of Castro, and a treaty was negotiated for signing in late October 1962. The Americans discovered what was afoot on 18 October, and Dean Rusk, Secretary of State, confronted Andrei Gromyko, informing him that the Americans knew everything. Khrushchev records the response:

> Gromyko answered like a gypsy who's been caught stealing a horse: It's not me, and it's not my horse. I don't know anything. Rusk said: We'll see this through to the end. Tell Khrushchev we wish he could prevent all this from occurring, but anything may happen (*Time*, 1 October 1990).

On 22 October, President Kennedy announced to the American people the discovery of the missiles, and warned Khrushchev that any attack from Cuba would be treated in the same way as an attack from the Soviet Union. He also imposed a naval blockade or quarantine to prevent any more missiles being transported to Cuba – though in fact all the Soviet missiles were already in place.

Castro claimed that he had reliable information that the Americans were going to launch an attack within a few hours and proposed a pre-emptive nuclear strike against the United States. Between 23 and 28 October Khrushchev and Kennedy exchanged letters. On 27 October, a US U2 reconnaissance aircraft was shot down by a Soviet missile, and the pilot, Major Rudolf Anderson, killed. The decision to shoot the aircraft down was taken by Soviet officers on Cuba and was not authorised by Moscow. However, those involved were only mildly reprimanded by Marshal Malinovsky, the Soviet Minister of Defence.

General Anatoly Gribkov, a Soviet officer involved in planning the deployment of the missiles on Cuba, stated in 1992 that the Soviets had secretly delivered twelve warheads for six FROG-7 short-range tactical nuclear launchers and had granted authority to the local Soviet commander, General Pliev, to fire the missiles if the Americans invaded. In 1994, however, he withdrew the assertion that General Pliev had had the authority to act unilaterally. He stated that in 1992 he had not had the authority to reveal that Marshal Malinovsky had forwarded highly secret coded messages to General Pliev on 22 and 27 October forbidding him to use any nuclear weapons without authority from Moscow. The United States was unaware that the Soviets had tactical nuclear weapons on Cuba at that time. The alert status of Soviet intercontinental ballistic missiles (ICBMs) and long-range nuclear bombers was increased from its routine peacetime status to the intermediate level, and then, for a short period during the crisis, to the state of combat readiness, when the nuclear warheads were mated to their missiles. In 1994 Lieutenant-Colonel Anatoly Dokuchaev stated that 162 nuclear warheads had been shipped to Cuba, consisting of 60 for the SS-4 and SS–5s, 12 for the FROG-7s, 80 for tactical cruise missiles, 6 gravity bombs and 4 nuclear naval mines.

With the situation very tense Khrushchev, without consulting Castro, accepted the solution proposed by President Kennedy. Soviet missiles were to be removed from Cuba in return for an assurance that the Americans and their allies would give a formal promise not to invade Cuba and that the United States would withdraw its Jupiter missiles from Turkey. Aleksandr Shelepin recounts that when Khrushchev came to the Politburo meeting to report this he was red in the face. 'Comrades, Lenin's cause is lost' (BBC TV, 13 December 1994), he said, revealing how humiliating he had found the climb down to be. Castro, in turn, was very annoyed, but the wounds of pride were healed six months later during a triumphal forty-day tour of the Soviet Union. Khrushchev had a horror of nuclear conflict and did not want war. His missiles, in the end, were bargaining chips and were used to strengthen Soviet security. Nevertheless, Pierre Salinger, Kennedy's press secretary, thought the world was only twenty-four hours away from nuclear war.

'THE PRESENT GENERATION OF SOVIET PEOPLE WILL LIVE UNDER COMMUNISM'

There were only two horses in the race to communism: the Soviet and the Chinese. Mao Zedong had claimed that China was ahead and this was one of the reasons behind the 'Great Leap Forward'. Khrushchev had to outdo the Chinese. At the Twenty-second Party Congress, in October 1961, he presented a new Party programme and named the date when the Soviet Union would enter the communist paradise. The economic goals were very ambitious as the Soviet Union in 1961 was a long way behind Uncle Sam, its role model. The programme was predicated on Soviet industrial growth of about 10 per cent annually, as well as a vast expansion of agriculture. It also assumed, erroneously, that the US economy was in terminal decline. On the basis of these assumptions, it was forecast that the USSR would surpass US gross and per capita production by 1970. A decade later and the USSR would have constructed, in the main, a communist society. In fact, of course, by the time 1980 arrived it was the Soviet Union which was in terminal decline.

In the never-ending search for accountability Khrushchev hit on a very useful notion. The new Party rules required each regular Congress to deselect at least one-quarter of the members of the CC and Presidium. Presidium members, as a rule, were not to serve for more than three terms. Those leaders who were indispensable could stay longer. The CCs of the republican Parties and *krai* and *oblast* committees were to replace at least one-third of the members at each regular election. Lower-level bodies were to change half the personnel. This meant, in practice, that an official could only serve a maximum of six years at the bottom level and fifteen at the top. This did not please those on the bottom rungs of the Party apparatus. A Party post was no longer a job for life. A CC plenum in November 1961 introduced an even less popular reform, the bifurcation of the Party apparatus. There were to be two halves, one responsible for industry, the other for agriculture. However, instead of improving the efficiency of the apparatus this change caused only frustration and discord. New state committees proliferated to such an extent that an official needed a chart to find his way round the maze.

De-Stalinisation was a major theme at the Twenty-second Congress. Khrushchev named the Anti-Party group for the first time. He also provided more gory details of the 1930s, and it was agreed to erect a monument to the victims. One of the most remarkable speeches was by D. Lazarkina, who had spent seventeen years in the Gulag.*. She informed incredulous delegates that Vladimir Ilich Lenin had appeared to her and made it quite clear that he did not like lying beside Stalin in the mausoleum. After this message from the other world, delegates had to agree to the removal of Stalin's body. They did not have the nerve to take it away and dispose of it but buried it nearby and put concrete on top. Later, a headstone with a simple inscription, I. V. Stalin, was erected. It is still there. However, Khrushchev did not take the next logical step and rehabilitate those who had lost out in the factional in-fighting against Stalin. It would be left to Gorbachev to bring Bukharin, for example, in from the cold. But the whole cultural climate was changing as those who had suffered began to put pen to paper. In 1962, books and articles and a large number of memoirs were published, among them Evgenia Ginsburg's *Into the Whirlwind*, a profoundly moving account of her travails.

One of the most influential novels was Alexander Solzhenitsyn's *One Day in the Life of Ivan Denisovich*, which was published in the literary journal *Novy Mir*, but only after the editor, Aleksandr Tvardovsky, had forwarded a copy to Khrushchev. Copies were also given to members of the Presidium. This time Khrushchev read the book for himself and resisted pressure from Mikhail Suslov and other conservatives to ban it. However, Nikita Sergeevich drew back from an open attack on Stalin. Addressing cultural workers on 8 March 1963 he spoke of Stalin's 'services' to the Party and his 'devotion' to Marxism and communism. Stalin, he explained, had been ill towards the end of his life and had suffered from paranoia. His crimes were due to his illness. Was this volte-face due to political pressure, or did Khrushchev fear that demolishing Stalin would eventually risk demolishing the Party?

CHURCHES AND CULTURE

Khrushchev's denunciation of Stalin's crimes made life easier for practising Christians, and Church life was more normal than at any time since the Revolution. Then began a vicious campaign which saw 10,000 churches and dozens of monasteries closed. The Monastery of the Caves, in Kiev, the most sacred place of the Orthodox faith, was one of them. Believers were harassed and imprisoned. It is still a mystery why Khrushchev singled out the Church, a soft target, for such treatment. He passed *One Day in the Life of Ivan Denisovich* for publication, yet it contains two memorable portraits of Christian believers in it. Khrushchev made it clear that under communism there was no room for religion. It remains a disgraceful episode, not only because it denied freedom of conscience, but also because it destroyed part of Russia's cultural heritage.

LABOUR POLICY

The rapid industrialisation of the Stalin era and war losses meant that the Soviet economy was always short of labour. Workers were always under pressure to work harder, and discovered that they could put pressure on management to make life more comfortable for themselves. Since enterprises were under constant pressure to meet plan targets, managers needed to keep their labour force. Gradually, managers colluded with workers to lower norms (work targets) and quality control, increase bonuses and improve conditions. Khrushchev was aware that labour morale was low and of the need to motivate workers to raise productivity. In April 1956 the draconian Stalinist labour laws of June 1940, which criminalised the changing of jobs and absenteeism, were repealed. Their effectiveness had been undermined by courts and managers declining to enforce them fully. Also the trade unions were reformed in 1957–58. During the 1930s they had lost their function of defending workers' rights and had turned into transmission belts to enforce higher targets. Now they were once again given a veto over managerial orders to sack workers and impose higher work quotas. Trade unions still did not represent the collective rights of their members against management and the government, but they were willing to take up some individual cases.

The wage reform of 1958–62 attempted to bring order to the chaotic wage structures. Hitherto it had been accepted that existing wages did not provide a living wage, so various subterfuges had to be resorted to. Now the minimum wage was raised and differentials between skilled and non-skilled were narrowed. It became difficult to pay workers bonuses unless the quality of work increased. Since many skilled workers were worse off as a result of the reform, various loopholes had to be found by management to pay them more lest they quit. The amount of money available for quality bonuses was so small as to have practically no effect. Although the reform addressed the problem of wage inequalities within an industry, it did not tackle the problem of inequalities between industries. The best-paid worker in the food industry, for example, earned about one-third of the wage of the best-paid worker in the coal or oil industries. Needless to say, workers left low-paid work to seek work in higher-paid industries. Unfortunately, in engineering many skilled workers were downgraded, especially machine tool operaters, one of the key sectors, and they left in droves. Often they took up semi-skilled or unskilled jobs as fitters (they assembled and repaired machines but did not operate them), where they earned more.

The crisis in engineering was only resolved after Khrushchev's removal, when a further reform measure allowed wages to rise rapidly and thereby solve the problem of recruiting enough machinists. Siberia and the Soviet Far East were rich in raw materials but the population was sparse. In the late 1950s, therefore, a campaign was launched to recruit young workers to move and settle in those often inhospitable regions. It was the industrial equivalent of the virgin lands. Incentives were provided, but it was one thing to recruit labour, quite another to keep it there. The major reason was the almost total lack of amenities. Many left before they completed their contracts, and overall the regions suffered a net loss of population.

Women made up almost half of the industrial labour force in the USSR, but were normally restricted to female-dominated industries – textiles, the garment industry, knitwear and food, where wages were low and the intensity of work very high. Where women were to be found in high-technology industries, such as chemicals or engineering, they were as a rule confined to the lower echelons and performed monotonous jobs. When jobs were mechanised, they were taken by men. On average, women earned two-thirds of men's wages, even when they had more education and experience. Soviet women had to cope with the double burden of running a home and family and working. They had to queue in their spare time, and few home chores were mechanised. Basic items such as eggs, pasta and even milk were sold unpackaged, and this involved waiting in the shop for everything to be measured, weighed and priced. There were normally three queues to be joined in each shop: one to identify the items, one to pay for them, and one to collect them. Supermarkets only came in under Gorbachev. Khrushchev tried to solve the labour shortage by drawing more and more women into production, but with limited success. Many women preferred staying at home to working in unpleasant surroundings for low pay, especially when child-care facilities were limited [26].

4 DECLINE AND FALL, 1963–64

The duties of office became even heavier as Khrushchev grew older. His son records him coming home, going for his usual walk, eating and then settling down with his files until midnight. He was back in the office at nine the next morning. He was an insatiable traveller, partly because he was hugely curious about the world and people but also because he was always on the look-out for better ways of doing things. In his last year in office he travelled a remarkable amount. This permitted the opposition to consolidate and plan his downfall.

In May 1964 he repaired to Egypt, where he was fêted by President Nasser and the Egyptian people. The main reason for being there was to inaugurate the Aswan High Dam. Nasser presented Khrushchev with his country's highest award, the Necklace of the Nile. What should he give Nasser? According to the USSR Supreme Soviet Presidium, the highest Soviet decoration was Hero of the Soviet Union. So Nasser was made Hero of the Soviet Union and, on Marshal Grechko's suggestion, the same honour was awarded to Marshal Hakim Amer. Andrei Gromyko nodded his approval, but in fact the awards were inappropriate, for both Nasser and Marshal Amer had supported Nazi Germany during the war. Apparently, Khrushchev announced the decision before it had been laid before the Presidium for its approval. Nikita Sergeevich did not lay great store by medals, decorations, titles and presents, but others did. He also ignored Nasser's very rough treatment of his own communists.

Khrushchev was oblivious of the fact that he was undermining his own position. He clearly regarded his posts as his for life. He had survived under Stalin by deploying great inter-personal skills but he now neglected or forgot them. One example was a trip to Poland in January 1964. He took along Kiril Mazurov, the Belorussian Party leader, of whom he had a high opinion. Later, back in Belorussia, they fell out over economic policy, and when Khrushchev got back to Moscow he informed the Presidium that a way had to be found to remove Mazurov. Khrushchev later cooled off, but the information got back to Mazurov and it turned him against the First Secretary.

Khrushchev first mused about retirement during the celebrations marking his seventieth birthday in April 1964. He had no successor in mind, for Frol Kozlov, who would have been his first choice, had suffered a stroke in April 1963 and never recovered. Another candidate was Aleksandr Shelepin, but he had refused to take over the Leningrad Party post because he saw it as demotion. Khrushchev did not have a high opinion of some of the others, especially Brezhnev.

THE PREPARATION OF THE *COUP*

The campaign to remove Khrushchev, according to Vladimir Semichastny, head of the KGB at the time, began in February 1964. Its genesis may have been the CC plenum in February. Podgorny, Brezhnev, Shelepin and Polyansky were the chief conspirators. Their task of discrediting Khrushchev was made easier by his blundering leadership style. At a CC plenum in July he indicated that the next reorganisation of agriculture would establish seventeen union-republican agricultural administrations based in Moscow, each of which would supervise the planning and procurement of a specified range of agricultural products. The Territorial Production Associations, set up in 1962, were to be abolished. This reform was to be adopted in November 1964, but it was ill advised economically (for example, meat and milk production have to be planned together, not by separate organisations), and was bound to be resented by local Party officials since it would return decision-making to the centre. In August, Khrushchev visited the virgin lands of Kazakhstan and again crossed swords with Baraev over fallow. Very angry, he sacked him on the spot, but after his departure the Party leader of the region convened his bureau and it found in favour of Baraev, who was reinstated. Such open dissent was unprecedented since 1957, and may have been covertly encouraged by the CC Secretariat. Then Khrushchev questioned the very existence of the USSR Academy of Sciences, and implied that a future CC plenum might have to consider its future.

Pyotr Shelest, a member of the Presidium and Party leader in Ukraine, dates the conspiracy against Khrushchev from 14 March 1964, his birthday. Podgorny and Brezhnev drove over to congratulate him. 'I had a premonition. ... They didn't quite trust me. They were sounding me out' [62 *p. 47*]. Similar soundings were being taken elsewhere. But all the time the cult of Khrushchev's personality was ascending new heights. His portraits got bigger and he was quoted as an authority on everything. Albums tracing Khrushchev's life were published, and the film *Our Nikita Sergeevich* was put on general release. During Khrushchev's seventieth birthday reception, eulogies to his wisdom reached new heights, with Brezhnev delivering the main speech.

Brezhnev was drafted into the CC Secretariat, while remaining President, when Kozlov fell ill. When it became clear that Kozlov would not recover, Khrushchev decided to move Brezhnev full-time into the Secretariat and made Anastas Mikoyan President. This offended Brezhnev, who loved the trappings of office. So keen was he to remain President that apparently he tried to remove Nikita Sergeevich there and then. According to Semichastny, Brezhnev came up with various ways of eliminating Khrushchev. One was by poisoning him. The idea of arranging for the plane bringing him back from Cairo to crash was also mulled over. Brezhnev thought of arranging a car accident and even of arresting him on the train coming back from Sweden. At the USSR Supreme Soviet meeting in July Khrushchev had wanted to introduce the five-day week. The conspirators feared this would make him popular and so they set about dissuading him. Aleksei Adzhubei, his son-in-law and editor-in-chief of *Izvestiya*, eventually convinced him that it was not opportune. Unwittingly, Adzhubei had aided the opposition. Then everyone went off on vacation to the Crimea. Brezhnev, now 'second secretary' and Khrushchev's deputy, went too. It was a perfect opportunity to talk to Party officials who were members of the Central Committee. By this time Nikita Sergeevich had alienated practically every elite in the country. Among those Brezhnev approached was Shelest.

> He didn't try to persuade me. He just sobbed, actually burst into tears. The man was an actor, a great actor. It sometimes got to the point, when he's downed a few drinks, that he'd climb on a chair and declaim something or other. Not Mayakovsky, of course, or Esenin, but some pun he'd thought up. ... [Khrushchev] swears at us, says we don't do a damn thing. Brezhnev sounded hurt, and there were tears in his eyes. ... We're thinking of calling a plenum and criticizing him a little. So what's the problem? Count me in favour [62 *pp. 78–9*].

Brezhnev was a very keen hunter and enjoyed duck shooting at Zavidovo, outside Moscow. However, in August 1964 his mind was not on duck hunting but on power. Gennady Voronov, then a member of the Presidium, sets the scene.

Everything had been under preparation for about a year. The threads led to Zavidovo, where Brezhnev usually went hunting. Brezhnev himself would put down a plus (next to the names of those who were ready to support him in the fight against Khrushchev) or minus. Each man would be worked on individually [62 *p. 82*].

In September, Khrushchev set off to inspect some military equipment, but his son, Sergei Nikitich, a weapons engineer, fell ill at the last moment and could not accompany him. Sergei Nikitich received a telephone call from Vasily Galyukov, an associate of Nikolai Ignatov, who had lost his position in the Party Presidium some years previously. Galyukov informed Sergei Nikitich that Ignatov was involved in a conspiracy against his father. In August, in Sochi, he had had many meetings with Party officials, and he always reported to Brezhnev.

KHRUSHCHEV BECOMES CARELESS

When his father returned, Sergei Nikitich informed him about the conversation.

Tell me again, whom did the man mention by name? he asked. Ignatov, Podgorny, Shelepin ... I began to repeat them, trying to be as precise as possible. Father thought for a moment. No, it's incredible. Brezhnev, Podgorny, Shelepin – they're completely different people. It can't be, he said thoughtfully. Ignatov – that's possible. He's very dissatisfied, and he's not a good man, anyway. But what can he do in common with the others? [62 *p. 108*].

The topic came up again the following evening. 'Evidently, what you told me is nonsense. I was leaving the Council of Ministers with Mikoyan and Podgorny, and I summarised your story in a couple of words. Podgorny simply laughed at me. "How can you think such a thing, Nikita Sergeevich?" Those were his actual words' [62 *p. 108*].
Khrushchev's naïvety is staggering. The obvious response would have been to ask Mikoyan to look into the allegations and report

back, but Nikita Sergeevich's political skills had deserted him. Why was this? His son suggests the following explanation.

He did not believe, he did not want to believe, that such a turn of events was possible. After all, the people accused had been his friends for decades! If he couldn't trust them, whom could he trust? What's more, my seventy-year-old father was tired, tired beyond measure, both morally and physically. He had neither the strength nor the desire to fight for power. Let everything take its course. I won't interfere, he had obviously decided [62 *p. 109*].

THE TRAP IS SPRUNG

Khrushchev went off with Mikoyan to Pitsunda in the Crimea for a rest. On 12 October a space launch was planned, and Leonid Smirnov, the Deputy Prime Minister responsible for missile technology, was, as usual, expected to phone immediately the spacecraft was in orbit. But he did not phone. Khrushchev became agitated and phoned him, berating him for being inefficient. It was clear that as far as the Deputy Prime Minister was concerned the transfer of power to Brezhnev and his co-conspirators had already taken place.

Mikhail Suslov phoned Khrushchev and informed him that the Presidium had convened and requested his presence. Under protest he agreed, but confided to Mikoyan that if he were the problem, he would go quietly. Brezhnev was on a visit to East Germany when he was told that Khrushchev had got wind of the plot. He did not want to return. He was to have phoned Khrushchev. 'It wasn't easy to talk him into it,' remarked Semichastny 'We had practically to drag him to the phone.' However, at the last moment, Brezhnev backed out and Suslov took over. He had only been apprised of the *coup* a week earlier since he was not a member of the Brezhnev-Podgorny nor the Shelepin group. When he was told of it he pursed his lips until they were blue and sucked in his cheeks. 'What are you talking about? This means civil war,' he responded. However, he soon joined in. Aleksei Kosygin was also told at the very end, according to Semichastny.

When they came to Kosygin about a week before, his first question was: Where does the KGB stand? When they told him that we were on board, he said: It's fine with me. As for Malinovsky, he was told with two days to go ... with only two days to go...!! Can you imagine that? [62 *p. 136*].

Khrushchev had one last official duty to perform. On the morning of 13 October, at Pitsunda, he received Gaston Palewski, the French minister of state, but for only half an hour.

BACK IN MOSCOW

Khrushchev and Mikoyan were met at Vnukovo 2 airport by Semichastny, who informed Nikita Sergeevich that everyone was waiting for him at the Kremlin. Why did Semichastny, the KGB chief, meet him?

> In the morning I called Leonid Ilich [Brezhnev]. Who's going to go to meet him? I asked. No one, you go by yourself, he replied. How can that be? I stammered. Under the present circumstances, he said slowly, why should everyone go? On the whole he was right. ... But won't he catch on? I asked a little worriedly. Just take some security and go, Brezhnev said, ending the conversation.

However, Semichastny had taken some precautions.

> I didn't even close the Kremlin to visitors. People were strolling around outside, while ... in the room the Presidium was meeting. I deployed my men around the Kremlin. Everything that was necessary was done. Brezhnev and Shelepin were nervous. I told them: Let's not do anything that isn't necessary. Let's not create the appearance of a coup.

That evening Brezhnev was still feeling nervous. He phoned Semichastny.

> Volodya, the meeting has just ended. Khrushchev is leaving. Where is he going? To his flat. But if he heads for the dacha? Let him go to his dacha. If he does that, what will you do? I've got everything ready, here, there and everywhere. We've anticipated everything. What if he phones? What if he calls in help? He's got no place to call. The whole communications network is in my hands. ... I've got the Kremlin lines, and the Party lines. If he wants to use the ordinary city phone, let him [62 *p. 150*].

There are no minutes of the two-day Presidium meeting, chaired by Khrushchev. The minutes of the CC plenum which dismissed

Khrushchev are extant. It is uncertain when Nikita Sergeevich decided to go. During the night of 13–14 October he phoned Mikoyan and said that he would not object if he were deprived of his offices.

I'm old and tired. Let them cope by themselves. I've done the main thing. Relations among us, the style of leadership, has changed drastically. Could anyone have dreamt of telling Stalin that he didn't suit us any more, and suggesting that he retire? Not even a wet spot would have remained where we had been standing. Now everything is different. The fear's gone. That's my contribution. I won't put up a fight [62 *p. 154*].

However, Pyotr Shelest kept his own record of the Presidium proceedings, in which he describes Khrushchev as 'dispirited and isolated'.

The Party brought us up and educated all of us, including me. ... You and I stand on common political and ideological ground, so I cannot fight you. I'll step down. I don't intend to fight. I ask you to forgive me if I ever offended anyone, if I allowed myself to behave rudely. ... I just want to say that I categorically reject some of the accusations made against me ... you, all of you present here, didn't tell me openly and honestly about my shortcomings. You were all yes men. ... I should like to make one request to the plenum [which would dismiss him]. He didn't manage to say [Shelest records] what his request was before Brezhnev cut him off. There will be no request. Suslov supported Brezhnev. Tears appeared in Nikita Sergeevich's eyes, and then he simply broke down and cried. It was sad to see. ... Polyansky had prepared the report to the plenum. The idea was for Brezhnev to give it, or at the very least, Podgorny. But Brezhnev simply funked it. ... And Podgorny also refused. ... I'd suggest Shelepin. He's got a way with words but he's too young. Then it was decided this way: Let Mikhail Andreevich [Suslov] give it. After all, he's our ideologist [62 *pp. 157–8*].

THE INDICTMENT

The CC plenum convened on 14 October, beginning at 6 p.m. Semichastny was surprised that there was no discussion. He was annoyed at the time but came to see the wisdom of it later. 'The

Presidium decided everything for the Central Committee, and having decided, prepared, chewed it over, and then chewed it over again, and threw it to the CC, saying, Vote!' [62 *p. 160*]. The Presidium report, delivered by Suslov, indicted Khrushchev on fifteen counts [*Doc. 19*]. It was the prosecution's case. There was not a word of thanks or praise for Nikita Sergeevich. Among other things he was accused of erratic leadership; of taking hasty and ill-considered decisions; of ignoring and slighting his colleagues; of developing his own personality cult; of turning Aleksei Adzhubei into a shadow foreign minister. Furthermore, Khrushchev was 'obsequious, incompetent and irresponsible' and had insulted Walter Ulbricht, the East German leader. The bifurcation of the Party apparatus which Khrushchev had initiated had caused much confusion. He had imagined he was an expert on everything that took his fancy, but industrial administration had become very complex and unwieldy, and his policies had reduced workers' welfare. He was often insensitive in dealing with foreign affairs and had thereby exacerbated tensions: on one occasion he referred to Mao Zedong as an 'old galosh', and on another, he told Todor Zhivkov, the Bulgarian leader, that all Bulgarians were parasites [*Doc. 19*]. Khrushchev was also said to have damaged foreign trade relations, and never to have met or telephoned the Minister of Foreign Trade. His campaigns against fallow and peasants' private plots and his support of the charlatan Trofim Denisovich Lysenko had cost agriculture dear [*Doc. 10*]. In addition, Khrushchev had promised and disbursed too much largesse to Third World states.

Many of these criticisms were justified. The plenum decided that the same person should never again simultaneously hold the position of First Party Secretary and Prime Minister. Mikoyan came to see Khrushchev to inform him about his future. The city flat and dacha were to be his for life. New bodyguards and domestic staff were to be assigned to him. He was to receive a pension of 500 roubles a month and a car. Mikoyan had suggested that Nikita Sergeevich be appointed consultant to the Presidium, but not surprisingly this was turned down. Before leaving, Mikoyan embraced and kissed Nikita Sergeevich. They were never to meet again.

5 THE UNWILLING PENSIONER, 1964–71

Nikita Sergeevich's dismissal wounded him mortally. He never came to terms with the shock of having his life's work overturned and the disgrace of becoming an 'unperson'. He was an idealist, and the dull weight of rejection crushed his spirit until his dying day. Even the devoted care of his wife, Nina Petrovna, did not reduce the pain. She suffered as much as he did but was better able to conceal it. Arbat, his daughter's Alsatian, knew that while Nikita Sergeevich was in office, he had no time for him. When Khrushchev returned after his dismissal Arbat went up to him and thereafter never left his side. The dog sensed that he now had all the time in the world for him.

Khrushchev had been dismissed while three Soviet cosmonauts were in orbit, and he had promised them a hero's welcome when they landed. The celebrations took place on 23 October, but Khrushchev could not bear to watch the occasion on television and took off for his dacha. However, Brezhnev and the others feared the worst – that he was heading for Red Square. The panic only subsided when the car changed direction and made for his dacha. Brezhnev ensured there would be no repeat and requested Nikita Sergeevich to move immediately to his dacha and not to come back to Moscow. His family could remain in the capital but would have to move to another flat.

Brezhnev summoned Khrushchev to the Central Committee to inform him about the conditions under which he was to live. It was to be their last meeting. One condition was that he was to move to another, more modest dacha in the country, at Petrovo-Dalnee. Both his Moscow flat and his dacha were bugged. It was all quite amateurish. The guards became so bored that they played music tapes, but the microphones in the walls became speakers. The walls were alive with the sound of music! The family became alarmed at Nikita Sergeevich's pessimism. He kept on repeating that his life was over, that life made sense only as long as people needed him. His doctor explained that this was one of the symptoms of shock.

THE MEMOIRS

Talk about the Memoirs began in 1966. With all the time in the world and such a wealth of experience he was ideally suited to write his autobiography, but Nikita Sergeevich never picked up a pen or pencil unless he could help it. The invention of the tape recorder solved the problem. The driving force behind the project was his son, Sergei Nikitich. Khrushchev refused to seek official aid, the use of a stenographer and so on. He was right, for the authorities would have killed the venture in its infancy. To begin with, he did not wish to dictate inside since he would be broadcasting everything to the KGB. However, outside also proved unsuitable because of overflying aircraft. In the end he moved back inside and thereby kept the KGB well informed. They did not prohibit his activities since they had no orders to do so, but reports were passed up the line for high-level consideration. Surprisingly, some time passed before attempts were made to scupper the whole operation.

Transcribing and editing eventually became the responsibility of Sergei Nikitich. Khrushchev dictated from memory – a phenomenal memory – and did not rely on sources. Especially startling were his recollections of the war, for he hardly got a fact wrong. This revealed how deeply the experience had engraved itself on his memory. He dictated best when he had an old acquaintance with him. He planned carefully. He went for long walks to think about the best ways of saying something. He avoided a chronological approach and hence flitted from topic to topic.

By 1968 Brezhnev felt confident enough to try to silence Khrushchev. He had no desire to meet Nikita Sergeevich face to face again, so Andrei Kirilenko was dispatched instead. Khrushchev was summoned to the CC building. Kirilenko, who would have won first prize for rudeness in the Politburo, ordered Khrushchev to hand over his Memoirs and stop dictating. A mere pensioner did not have the right to record the history of the Party and the state. Nikita Sergeevich categorically refused, getting angrier by the minute.

You can take everything away from me: my pension, the dacha, the flat. That's all within your power, and it wouldn't surprise me if you did. So what? – I can still make a living. I'll go back to being a metalworker – I still remember how it's done. If that doesn't work out, I'll put on my rucksack and go begging. People will give me what I need.

He looked at Kirilenko.

But no one would give you a crust of bread. You'd starve ... you violated the constitution ... when you stuck listening devices all over the dacha. Even in the toilet – you spend the people's money eavesdropping on my farts [72 *p. 247*].

Kirilenko, who was no match for Khrushchev, scored a partial victory. Nikita Sergeevich recorded very little in 1968. The episode so alarmed him that he began discussing how to get the tapes and transcripts abroad. They could be published in retaliation for some action against him, if need be. It turned out to be relatively simple to get them into a foreign bank vault. Those passages regarded as too inflammatory were excised from the first American edition in 1971, and only published in 1990. Brezhnev and the KGB did not relent, and tried various techniques to extract the Memoirs from Nikita Sergeevich.

Yury Andropov took over the KGB and Sergei Nikitich had some faith in him. He therefore handed over the existing text on 11 July 1970. There were 2,810 typewritten pages and the typists had another 929. His father was in hospital, and it was agreed that the materials would be returned when he left, but this was never in fact done, since the KGB stated that everything had been passed on to the CC at its request. Sergei Nikitich had been neatly out-manoeuvred and Nikita Sergeevich never forgave his son for turning over the materials to the KGB. When it was announced that the Memoirs would be published in the United States, Khrushchev was hauled in front of Arvid Pelshe, chairman of the Party Control Commission (the Party's own police). Eventually he signed a statement that his Memoirs were incomplete and that he had not sent them abroad. Both statements were technically correct. Not all of his memoirs had been smuggled abroad so they were incomplete. He personally had not sent them out of the country because this had been done by others.

The official business over, Khrushchev could not resist the temptation to pour scorn on the limited achievements of his successors. He derived great pleasure from pointing out that Soviet agriculture was in such a mess that grain had annually to be imported from the United States. Nikita Sergeevich paid a price for his outburst. He suffered a mild heart attack and had to return to hospital. When he returned home at the end of 1970 a rapid decline set in. He could no longer walk very far without resting on a folding stool he always took with him. Arbat had carried it but he was now gone. Khrushchev began dictating again in February but he was no longer his old self. In particular, he was dissatisfied with his recollections on cultural policy. In January 1971, the KGB had contacted Sergei Nikitich and invited him to check the Russian retranslation of the English published edition. This was strange since they could surely have checked it against the original Russian in the possession of the CC. Progress Publishers then brought out the Russian translation, but it was stamped 'for official use only'.

At last the Soviet establishment became acquainted with what Khrushchev had said. When volume two of the Memoirs came out in America in 1974 Sergei Nikitich was again contacted by the KGB, who wanted him to sign a letter declaring the Memoirs to be a forgery. This posed a slight difficulty since he had not seen the second volume. He consulted his mother, Nina Petrovna, and she pointed out logically that one could not state that a book was a forgery if one had not read it. Sergei Nikitich demanded to see a copy for himself and his mother, whereupon the KGB conceded that they had not seen a copy either! So a letter was signed stating that the Memoirs were incomplete and that Khrushchev had no idea how they had ended up abroad. When Brezhnev died in November 1982 Sergei Nikitich thought of asking his successor, Yury Andropov, to return the tapes and transcripts. When he finally got round to sending a letter, Mikhail Gorbachev was leader and he agreed immediately to their return. But this was more easily said than done. Almost two years passed, filled with the usual excuses: the archives were undergoing restoration; they were being moved to another building; and so on. Finally, in August 1988, the exciting news arrived that they were ready. Disappointment was in store. Only 400 pages were in the folder. What about the rest? It transpired that the CC was holding about 6,000 pages, but glasnost helped resolve the matter. The American publisher returned all the materials they had to Sergei Nikitich. Other sources had been hidden away in the Soviet Union. Work could now begin on the definitive Russian edition of the Memoirs.

THE END

Khrushchev's seventy-seventh birthday was celebrated at Petrovo-Dalnee on 17 April 1971. He was in sombre mood, as his doctor had forbidden him to do any gardening, which had been one of his delights. Many of his agricultural innovations had first been tried out in his garden. It was the last family gathering at Petrovo-Dalnee.

In July, black melancholy overtook Nikita Sergeevich and he spoke of suicide. The last comments he dictated tell the story.

My time has passed and I am very tired. I am at an age when I have nothing before me but my past. My only future is to go to the grave. I want to die. It is so dull – so dull and boring for me to live in my situation. But I did want this opportunity to express my opinion one last time [60 *p. 203*].

On 5 September Nina Petrovna and Khrushchev intended to visit their daughter Rada, her husband Aleksei Adzhubei and the family. But his heart began to trouble him. During the night he suffered a massive heart attack, and he died on 11 September 1971. CC officials confiscated from the dacha all Khrushchev's private papers and other materials they regarded as important. The CC also decided that Khrushchev's death be announced at 10 a.m. on Monday, 13 September. The wake would begin at the same time in a suburban hospital, and the funeral would be at noon in Novodevichy cemetery. This would ensure that many who wished to attend would hear too late. The CC agreed to pay all funeral expenses, but no one from the Politburo phoned his condolences. Khrushchev remained a Party member to the last, and the CC sent a wreath: 'To Comrade N. S. Khrushchev from the CC, CPSU, and the USSR Council of Ministers.' One arrived at the very last moment: 'To Nikita Sergeevich Khrushchev from Anastas Ivanovich Mikoyan.' Mikoyan's son, Sergo, had not informed his father of Khrushchev's death. He learned about it only from that morning's *Pravda*. In fact, his presence at the funeral might have been very embarrassing for the authorities.

Nina Petrovna Khrushcheva was moved to a dacha in Zhukovka, and the one in Petrovo-Dalnee was demolished. She had always expressed a wish to be buried beside her husband, but when she died in August 1984 Konstantin Chernenko was Party leader. There was obviously no point in approaching him for permission, but fortunately he was on holiday and Mikhail Gorbachev was in charge in Moscow. A request was made and permission was granted within 90 minutes.

All traces of Khrushchev had now disappeared except his grave, so Sergei Nikitich determined to erect a headstone which would serve as a monument. He was advised that the only sculptor who could do justice to the subject was Ernst Neizvestny. He hesitated, since his father and the sculptor had rowed in the past. He need not have worried. Neizvestny respected his father for his achievements, and was only concerned how best to represent his successes and failures [*Doc. 20*]. Permission to erect the monument was given by Aleksei Kosygin, and by September 1975, after four years of endeavour, it was in place.

PART THREE: ASSESSMENT

6 COURAGEOUS FAILURE

The collapse of the Soviet Union in 1991 brought to an end the Soviet experiment. It had boldly attempted to fashion a new type of society, one based not on competition but on cooperation. The market economy had been rejected as the key to resource allocation and a planned economy introduced. Without market mechanisms bureaucrats had to intervene to guide the economy forward, but as the economy grew so did the need for more and more bureaucrats. Eventually, a vast edifice was constructed which superimposed itself on production. It consisted of two parts: the ministerial or governmental, and the Party apparatus. Ministries, of course, exist in a market economy, since intervention by the state to regulate affairs is necessary.

Lenin conceived of the ministries and economic committees running the economy and the state. What then was to be the role of the Communist Party? It was to have overall supervisory powers, to provide the inspiration and drive which would move everything forward. But Lenin forgot something. The struggle for power also exists under socialism. Stalin was strong in the Party apparatus but his competitors for Lenin's mantle were ensconced in governmental offices. Stalin therefore built up the Party apparatus until he had won the race for power and then concentrated on his own apparatus which, in turn, was based on three pillars: the government, the Party, and the political police (NKVD). Stalin attempted to make everyone accountable to him. He was the managing director of USSR Co. Ltd. This resulted in ministries and ministers becoming increasingly important.

In 1934, a People's Commissar [Minister] could be censured for his 'professorial' manners. Five years later, it was not their allegedly 'proletarian' work-style but their diplomas for which the officials received loud praise. The way was free for the introduction of grades, insignia, and even uniforms for different categories of officials which began in 1938 and attained its apogee after the war when it was proposed that university graduates wear a specific badge [119 *p. 24*].

However, the enormous pressures applied to increase output in the 1930s forced ministries and enterprises to defend themselves against failure. They colluded, and gradually made it more and more difficult for Moscow to have its way. The war reinforced this process. There was an enormous expansion of ministries after the war, and in the late 1940s Stalin's decisions were only implemented when they also accorded with the interests of the ministries. One scholar has argued that in order for a policy to be implemented the Presidium had either to make sure that it coincided with ministerial interests or to amend those interests by restructuring those ministries. However, it proved extremely difficult to rearrange the interests of ministries. They had a tendency gradually to regroup since the bureaucratic culture was so developed. Khrushchev ruefully admitted in 1958: 'The main force was administrative action, from one centre, all over the country. It was really incredible. A minister used to be higher than God. ... The Party, the trade unions, and the members of the Young Communist League were only like auxiliaries' [119 *p. 25*]. This is a very telling admission and was expressed after the *sovnarkhoz* reform of 1957 which had attempted to break up the central power of the ministries. It explains why this reform attempt was bound to fail.

Khrushchev, like Gorbachev, was aware that the Soviet Union faced various crises when he took over. Stalin's legacy was a powerful state, a leading world power, a cowed, resentful population, and lagging industrial and agricultural productivity. Unlike Gorbachev, who needed two years to perceive the need for economic and political reform to go hand in hand, Khrushchev realised this from the very beginning. The key problem was productivity. How was the average industrial and farm worker to be motivated so as to perform better? Stalinism had caused personal initiative to wither. How was it to be revitalised? Khrushchev was attempting to transform society in order to make it more efficient and to enable the Communist Party to be more effective in running the country. But this meant pursuing policies that were mutually opposed. One was to liberate society in order to make it more productive. The other was to bring it under closer Party control. However, the bureaucrats who were to administer this new society had acquired their skills and positions under Stalin. In other words, Khrushchev had to de-Stalinise without destroying some of the pillars of Stalinism: the planned economy, collectivised agriculture, Party control of culture and intellectual life, and the political monopoly of the Communist Party. He chose to reform without using coercion, but this emboldened his opponents to risk opposing him. Filtzer [26] identifies four main reasons why Khrushchev's reforms failed:

1   Some reforms failed because they were badly thought out or poorly prepared, even where they were well intentioned and addressed real difficulties. Khrushchev, especially in the later years of his rule, was constantly being accused of pursuing 'hare-brained schemes'.
2   Some reforms failed because the Soviet system could not 'digest' them. In other words, the cumbersomeness of the Soviet bureaucracy and the country's economic backwardness undermined the new policies and either prevented their implementation or distorted their results.
3   Some reforms failed because sections of the Communist Party or government bureaucracy felt threatened by them and resisted or distorted their implementation.
4   Finally, some reforms failed because Khrushchev and the rest of the Communist Party leadership, like the officials below them, were willing to liberalise economic and political life only in so far as this did not threaten their own ruling position. Thus the policies they followed were not nearly as radical as what was actually needed to solve the problems the country faced.

Usually, individual reforms failed because of a combination of two or more of these reasons. This, in turn, created more problems, which led to further attempts at reform. There are exceptions. Some reforms were wholly successful – for example, the ending of the Stalinist Gulag, the labour camps, and the release of millions of prisoners. Other reforms were of fundamental significance – such as the bringing of the NKVD (KGB) under Party and state control. The intelligentsia, with whom Khrushchev fought a running battle, always regarded Khrushchev's contribution to Soviet life as positive because of this reform.

After Stalin's death it was inevitable that there would be reform. The first to grasp the nettle were Beria and Malenkov. Beria was very innovative and was probably the best-informed member of the Party Presidium. The nature of Soviet politics required him to build up his 'tail' and to adopt policies which would increase economic efficiency and popular support. Public opinion becomes important as it affects the legitimacy of the regime. He introduced rapid change in agriculture and nationality affairs, started looking for solutions to the Korean, Yugoslav and German problems, and began emptying the Gulag.

Khrushchev found it easier to come up with reforms in agriculture than industry. This was because the centre never devised efficient plan-fulfilment criteria. Physical planning meant that success indicators were expressed in weight, roubles, square metres and so on. If the plan was in tonnes it was rational for the enterprise to produce very heavy goods, irrespective of the demand for them. If it was expressed in roubles, the plant chose to produce very expensive products and neglect cheap items, such as nuts and bolts. This then led to a shortage of nuts and bolts. Often, most of the parts of a product were produced but the finishing item was not: shoes had no laces, there were not enough spokes for wheels, and so on. Enterprises were wary of technological innovation, since during the settling-in period production could suffer and everyone be penalised. Management needed to retain the goodwill of workers, who could not be fired except for grave breaches of discipline. If new technology implied redundancies it became even less attractive. Even if everyone had done their job according to the plan the economy would still have been inefficient, since no central planning organisation could cope with the millions and millions of decisions which had to be taken.

Khrushchev's bold initiative to overcome the above deficiencies and the power of ministries was to launch the *sovnarkhoz* reform of February 1957. Enterprises were no longer under the authority of ministries but of regional economic councils. The belief was that a regional council could efficiently coordinate production and distribution of those enterprises within its region. Under the former system, a factory's inputs could come from the other end of the country when in fact the plant next door could have supplied some of them. The reason for this was that the neighbouring enterprise was under a different ministry. Each ministry had its own supply and distribution network and had little incentive to coordinate its efforts with other ministries. Transport costs, as a result, were needlessly high. Often a plant would suffer a shortage while a nearby one had a surplus. Now plants would obtain their supplies from within their own region.

The main weakness of this reform was that it left the basic

planning system intact. The competition between ministries for investment was replaced by that of regional councils. Each council tried to become autarkic or self-sufficient. But since, in fact, no region was autarkic, an enterprise had to deal with a myriad of regional economic councils in order to obtain its inputs. Councils now accorded preference to their own enterprises, but this involved trying to make many of the parts that had previously come from outside the region. The result was a bureaucratic nightmare, and Moscow's solution was predictable. New bureaucratic planning networks were established to overcome the localism of the regional councils. State Committees, Central Councils, a Supreme Economic Council and a strengthened State Planning Commission (Gosplan) were introduced [26]. The regional councils were concentrated in larger regional councils. The State Committees gradually began to act as ministries. Instead of reducing the bureaucracy managing industry, by 1963 it had almost tripled. Duplication increased, innovation declined and the stock of unwanted goods grew.

The *sovnarkhoz* reform failed not merely because it was not well thought through but because the bureaucratic planning system virtually doomed it to failure. Competition between ministries in Moscow in the battle to achieve plan goals and attract more investment was merely transferred to the regional level. Just as each ministry paid little attention to the damage it was doing to other ministries, so the regional councils looked after their own enterprises and did not pause to consider the costs to other councils. Not surprisingly, this reform was one of the first to be reversed after Khrushchev's removal. Recentralisation was seen as the answer, but the endemic inefficiency of the planning system could not be overcome under Brezhnev or even Gorbachev. Agriculture reforms suffered the same fate. Agricultural ministries were abolished or restructured and decision-making devolved to regional bodies such as the Territorial Production Associations. Again recentralisation was readopted in 1964.

The Khrushchev era marks the beginning of the deep division in the Communist Party on how the economy should be run. The conservatives – Molotov, Kaganovich and others – favoured tight central control through ministries, while the innovators – Beria, Malenkov and Khrushchev – wanted enterprises to acquire greater control over their activities, thereby weakening ministerial control. The bureaucratic confusion of the late Khrushchev period promoted the view that the way ahead was to set up even more central ministries. However, Aleksei Kosygin, who became Prime Minister in October 1964 and was a technocrat, was wary of this solution. At the October 1964 plenum he spoke of the need to increase Party control over economic and social life. Hence, when the ministries were re-established, attempts were made to ensure that they behaved differently and became more accountable than their predecessors in 1957.

The apogee of de-Stalinisation was reached in 1961, at the Twenty-second Party Congress, when Khrushchev delivered a more direct, and public, condemnation of Stalin, blaming him for the unpreparedness of the Soviet Union when the Germans attacked in June 1941, and for inept leadership. The members of the Anti-Party group were also publicly identified. The symbolic act of removing Stalin from the Lenin-Stalin mausoleum signalled the resurrection of Lenin as the only source of communist authority. There was great expectancy about the future, and rumours that Stalin's victims (but not Trotsky) would be rehabilitated. These changes did not take place, however. On the contrary, in 1963 Stalin got a better press from Khrushchev and the censor became stricter. The pressure of the Chinese led to the communist dawn being announced and a new Party programme promised the world. The concern about the Chinese led to many jokes. One involves a West German driving his new Mercedes in East Germany. He tries to overtake an old banger but every time he tries it accelerates and disappears. Eventually he meets the driver in a lay-by. 'Tell me, how is it possible for your old car to beat my new Mercedes?' 'Simple,' is the reply. 'The front wheels are Russian and the back ones are Chinese!'

The ups and downs of de-Stalinisation were, of course, closely linked to the vicissitudes of political and economic reform. After July 1957 Khrushchev could press ahead, but the qualified success of his economic reforms caused widespread dissatisfaction among the population. It also strengthened the views of the conservatives, who believed that his reforms were undermining the authority of the institutions which were vital to the running of the state – namely, the government and the Communist Party. He was also weakening the authority of the ideology, Marxism-Leninism, which was the glue which kept the whole system together. The ending of the infallibility of the Party at the Twentieth Party Congress increased the risk that lack of economic success would erode the Party's authority. The price rises of 1962 had led to strikes, demonstrations and deaths. Khrushchev's colleagues began to fear for the stability of the country.

De-Stalinisation was a stop-go policy, closely linked to events in other policy areas. One of these was foreign affairs, where the demolition of Stalin was bound to have a dramatic impact on eastern Europe and the rest of the communist world. The uprising in the GDR in June 1953 contributed partly to Beria's fall, but it was an ominous reminder that communist regimes in eastern Europe lacked legitimacy. The attempt to resolve the conflict with the Yugoslavs ran the risk of making Yugoslav socialism more attractive to the east Europeans. This had been the reason for the original breach in 1948.

The Hungarian disaster of 1956 could be blamed on de-Stalinisation, and the use of military force – words having failed – to put it down was a watershed in post-war politics. Not only did it put back the cause of de-Stalinisation, and hence reform, in eastern Europe, but it also weakened the Soviet Union abroad. Communist parties in western Europe lost many members and declined in influence except in France and Italy. One of the consequences was that the political and cultural thaw in the Soviet Union came to an end. The conflict with the Chinese, who took great exception to de-Stalinisation, led to an open breach in the late 1950s. The world communist movement now became polycentric.

However, it was the relationship with the United States which caused the most concern. Khrushchev advocated co-existence, but the 'spirit of Geneva' was dissipated in Paris in 1960. The weakness of the GDR regime necessitated a solution to the Berlin problem, and since the West stood firm the Wall went up. This was a very poor advertisement for socialism. Likewise, the Cuban missile crisis flowed from Cuban weakness and the lack of Soviet ICBMs. One of the casualties was the cultural thaw of 1962, which saw some remarkable writing published.

The volte-face of 1963 seems to be linked to failure in foreign affairs, the criticisms of the Chinese and the lack of economic success which had led to bloodshed at Novocherkassk. The partial rehabilitation of Stalin was the nadir and was forced on Khrushchev. The Soviet élite had brought home to the First Secretary that de-Stalinisation was threatening their hold on power. The more money spent on defence, the less there was for other pursuits. Significantly, among the points of his indictment in October 1964, military, security and foreign affairs hardly surface. He had lost the battle to restrict defence spending and with it the expansion of the military-industrial complex.

Khrushchev faced a series of dilemmas and they can be summarised as follows [26]:

1   He had to do away with the worst excesses of the Stalinist system: the arbitrary secret police; the competitive infighting among vested interests inside the Communist Party; the empire-building and bureaucratic conservatism of the ministries.

2   He had to motivate the population by making them feel they no longer had to live in fear, that living standards would rise, and that the system would become more open. He wanted workers and peasants now to feel that they had a stake in the system.

3   He had to do all this without fundamentally changing the system. Thus, there would still be a Communist Party, which would continue to determine how the country was run. There would still be a large bureaucracy, but it would be run more efficiently and humanely and with more committed people. There would still be managers of factories and collective farms, and they would continue to enjoy substantial privileges.

In short, the Soviet system would remain, and would continue to be based on the principle that those in charge, be they Communist Party officials, government administrators or economic managers, would exist as a privileged group relative to the rest of the population. However, the system would become more fair and responsive to the needs and wishes of ordinary citizens. But these ordinary people would not acquire political power. They would not be able to change the personnel who ruled them – that would still be decided by the élites themselves. Khrushchev wanted to make Communist Party rule more effective and thereby more secure. He wanted to make every official accountable to him, to the Party and to the people. However, this meant changing the *modus operandi* of many officials. It also meant a rotation of cadres, with the more effective being upwardly mobile. Khrushchev wanted to break the power of patronage and replace it with objective criteria, such as effectiveness. However, this was bound to send a shiver down many bureaucratic spines. While many feared for their positions, others feared for the rule of the Party. Khrushchev, in fact, never attempted to change the system but only certain of its features. He left it to those in place to implement reform, but in many cases reform meant reducing their own power and privilege. One of the consequences of victory of the Party over the governmental apparat in July 1957 was the increased prestige of Party officials. This, paradoxically, was to contribute to Khrushchev's downfall in 1964. Enormous efforts were undertaken to canvass the support of *oblast* and *krai* Party secretaries so that there would be a rock-solid majority in the Central Committee for his removal.

It might be argued that the logic of the Soviet system defeated Khrushchev. Given a planned economy, the power of the ministries could not be restricted without increasing inefficiency. The only way to cut the ministries down to size would have been to introduce market mechanisms, but Khrushchev was ideologically blind to the advantages of the market. He therefore gave more power to the bureaucracy, which was bound to expand as the Soviet system grew and became more complex.

Could the Stalinist system have been reformed and still retain its salient characteristics? Khrushchev thought so, and so did Gorbachev. One of the lessons the latter drew from Khrushchev's experience was that reform had to be bold and daring, since slow reform would be choked by the bureaucracy. However, Gorbachev's failure suggests that the Stalinist system was an historical phenomenon which flourished in a given context, at a certain time, but was not economically dynamic enough to satisfy the needs of the people. Had Gorbachev been economically successful it is conceivable that he could have overcome the nationality problems and held a renewed Soviet Union together. By contrast, his failure seemed to vindicate the belief of Khrushchev's conservative critics – Molotov and Kaganovich in the lead – that the process of reform would eventually unravel the entire Soviet system. A Soviet Union under Beria might have arrived at the same conclusions as Khrushchev, but Beria was more pragmatic and lacked Khrushchev's faith in the Utopia of communism. Beria might have inaugurated a mixed economy, run by a socialist government. However, this would have restricted his power. Had Molotov become Party leader in July 1957, he would have been conservative in policy. Lacking direct expertise in industry or agriculture, he would have relied on others. The industrial lobby would have grown stronger, and as he opposed the *rapprochement* with Yugoslavia or concessions to the West and the Chinese, his foreign policy would have required high defence spending. Eventually, the inherent inefficiencies of the Soviet economy would have become obvious. The reality is that the Stalinist system was strong enough to sustain the first wave of attacks by Khrushchev but had deteriorated to such an extent that by the Gorbachev era it collapsed when put under pressure.

What was Khrushchevism? One answer is the erratic, impulsive, inspirational, innovative and restlessly questing leadership of Nikita Sergeevich. Another is the Utopian belief in the dawn of communism; the conviction that the Stalinist system could be made more effective without fundamentally changing it; that workers and managers would perform better if motivated by the freedom to shape their working lives. Above all, it was based on faith in the universal victory of communism. This led Khrushchev to take risks in foreign policy because he was convinced of final victory. Stunned by the riches of America, he informed the Americans: 'We'll bury you!' Khrushchevism is normally regarded as a negative term, yet it was Khrushchev's successors who presided over the slow decline of the country. He, at least, tried to find solutions. The drift of this analysis is that he was in a no-win situation.

PART FOUR: DOCUMENTS

DOCUMENT 1   KAGANOVICH AND THE PURGES

Khrushchev relates a story about how Kaganovich unearthed enemies of the people in Ukraine. Although Kaganovich had been Khrushchev's patron at one time relations between them were not very friendly.

Kaganovich described how he had gathered the party's most loyal members together in the Kiev opera house, where he questioned each one individually, insisting 'Let's have it, who knows what about any enemies of the people?' It was a ludicrous kind of people's court. Yet people came forth and said anything they could think of.

As Kaganovich told us, he found out that there was one woman whose last name was Nikolaenko – a party member, an active worker on the cultural front. She was supposedly fighting against enemies of the people but received no support. Kaganovich was only too glad to help. He summoned the woman Nikolaenko, who came and began to identify enemies of the people. The consequences for those she named were devastating.

Today it is shameful to recount, but it really happened. This is why I want to tell what I know, so that such despicable acts never happen again. Yet at the time, all this madness was seen in a positive way.

Kaganovich told the story to Stalin, and at some meeting Stalin said that there were small people who made huge contributions to the cause of our party. One such person was this woman Nikolaenko, in the Ukraine, who had helped the party to uncover the enemy in a big way. The anecdote found its way into the press. Nikolaenko was immediately placed on a pedestal as a fighter for the revolution against enemies of the people.

Nikita Khrushchev [60], p. 34.

DOCUMENT 2   KHRUSHCHEV AND STALIN

Stalin was constantly being fed false information about colleagues and had to devise ways of attempting to discern the truth.

'No, I didn't know,' I answered.

'He had some evidence of some kind against you,' said Stalin, staring into my eyes with that blank look of his.

I stared back at him, not knowing what to say. Then I answered, 'No, I did not know Antipov was arrested, nor do I know with what he has been charged. But I do know that Antipov would not, indeed could not, offer any evidence against me, because I never have anything to do with him. The extent of our acquaintance is tipping our hats in the hall and our work together at party meetings.'

Stalin turned, lowered his head, and started to talk about Moscow, the real reason he had called me in the first place. He asked me some questions, As he did so I think he was trying to read in my eyes how I was going to act. It just so happened that my external appearance, my face and my eyes, gave him no reason to suspect any link between me and Antipov. Well, what if – after all, it's entirely subjective – he had somehow gotten the impression that I was trying to hide something? Would it only have been a matter of time, then, until we had a new enemy of the people?

We walked a bit more, and then he said he had no more questions for me; so I left. Later, of course, I couldn't stop thinking about the questions he had asked me. I felt like asking what basis Stalin had for coming after me like that. The explanation lies in his utter irresponsibility and complete lack of respect for anyone other than himself.

Ibid., p. 37.

DOCUMENT 3   STALIN AND DEFENCE

Khrushchev reveals how concerned Stalin was about war. The defensiveness of the Soviet Union led Stalin to become oversensitive about discussing military technology. This became worse towards the end of his life.

In the days leading up to Stalin's death, we believed that America would invade the Soviet Union and we would go to war. Stalin trembled at this prospect. How he quivered! He was afraid of war.

He knew that we were weaker than the United States. We had only a handful of nuclear weapons, while America had a large arsenal of nuclear arms. Of course, in other areas – conventional forces and ground forces – we had the advantage.

Stalin never did anything that might provoke a war with the United States. He knew his weakness. This fear stayed with him from the first days of World War II, when he said: 'Lenin left us a state and we turned it to shit.' Our victory in the war did not stop him from trembling inside.

Stalin insisted on absolute secrecy and no discussion whatsoever about weapons. If anybody showed an interest in weapons, Stalin believed he had switched his allegiance and been recruited as an agent. Stalin would say the reason for that person's interest was his desire to inform his 'real masters' – the catchphrase we used at that time for enemies. The arrests started again, and soon the prisons were overflowing. Many of those arrested were former prisoners of war who had returned home. However, they did not return to their apartments or their collective or state farms; they were sent to camps. They worked in Siberia, Kolyma and other remote areas.

Ibid., pp. 100–1.

DOCUMENT 4   KHRUSHCHEV AND NUCLEAR WEAPONS

Khrushchev was besotted with rockets, missiles and 'war toys'. His son, Sergei, was a weapons engineer and they had many discussions.

While Stalin was alive he gave military questions much thought. But I believe that our greatest advances in defense have come about since he died. The main reason is that after the war, industry grew very quickly. Second, we had a better understanding of the new directions being taken in military industry. From that it follows that we could invest in the areas that would produce the most effective weapons.

We set as our goal the development of an atomic-powered military submarine fleet capable of launching both nuclear and non-nuclear missiles. We developed intercontinental missiles and strategic rockets with ranges of two and four thousand kilometers. We also developed short-range weapons carried by infantrymen that could launch either nuclear or non-nuclear missiles. Nuclear weapons were the main thing that increased our military might.

Ibid., p. 71.

DOCUMENT 5   **POLAND**

The situation in Poland in 1956 became very tense, but civil war did not break out. Poland was of great significance to Moscow because of its troops in the GDR. It is interesting that Khrushchev takes for granted the fact that a Soviet delegation can provide false explanations of events. Another reason why Gomulka wanted Soviet troops to stay may have been his unease at the prospect of having to rely on the Polish armed forces in times of emergency. No Polish communist leader ever felt secure, since they were always aware of the danger posed by Polish nationalism.

(i) Then we learned about developments in Warsaw [in October 1956]: the Soviet Union was being reviled with abusive language and the government was close to being over-thrown. The people rising to the top were those whose mood was anti-Soviet. This might threaten our lines of communication and access to Germany through Poland. Therefore, we decided to take certain measures to maintain contact with our troops in the German Democratic Republic.

We decided to send a delegation to Poland and have a talk with the Polish leadership. They recommended that we not come. Their reluctance to meet with us heightened our concern even more. So we decided to go there in a large delegation. I was the head. There were Mikoyan, Bulganin, Molotov, Kaganovich, Marshal Konev, and others.

We landed at the airport and were met by Ochab and Gomulka. The meeting was cool. You could see great concern on the face of Ochab. We began speaking harshly in raised voices. Ochab boiled up even more and said with anger. 'Why are you blaming me? I'm not the Central Committee secretary anymore. Ask them.' He pointed to Gomulka and the others.

The situation in Poland grew even more difficult. We did not know what to do. We were more afraid than ever that a leadership would arise that would be anti-Soviet. We did not want the relations to return to what they had been before the war, when Poland had a bourgeois leadership.

During our talks in Warsaw, Gomulka made an anxious but sincere declaration: 'Poland needs friendship with the Soviet Union more than the Soviet Union needs friendship with Poland. Can it be that we failed to understand our situation? Without the Soviet Union we cannot maintain our borders with the West. We are dealing with our internal problems, but our relations with the Soviet Union will remain unchanged. We will still be friends and allies.' He said all this with such intensity and such sincerity that I believed his words. When we met alone, I said to our delegation, 'I think there is no reason not to believe Comrade Gomulka.'

We explained that the reason our troops were on the move to Warsaw was in conjunction with manoeuvres that would be taking place. Nobody believed this false explanation, but everybody was pleased by the fact that an explanation was given.

Ibid., pp. 114–16.

(ii) To my surprise and amazement, Comrade Gomulka objected sharply and argued the case for having our troops remain in Poland. I was surprised because I still carried in my memory how the Poles had vilified us in 1956. The Soviet Union really got it then, especially the army. There was even a demand that Rokossovsky be recalled. Gomulka said then, 'You must understand that under present circumstances there is no trust in Comrade Rokossovsky. So it would be better if he returned to the Soviet Union.' He came back, and here he received a medal and a hero's welcome. We valued highly the service Comrade Rokossovsky gave in the war. He was of Polish descent himself, and a Communist, a good, honest fighting man. He possessed all the qualities of a modern progressive man and a modern military figure. Of course, no one [in Poland] trusted him. Although he was a Pole, he was not a Polish Pole, but a Soviet Pole. Everyone thought he would conduct policy in Poland with the interests of the Soviet Union in mind.

I began to rack my brain trying to figure out why Gomulka objected to our withdrawing our troops. From the point of view of Soviet strategy and the strategy of the socialist countries, there was nothing to justify the presence of our troops in Poland. They cost us a lot to maintain there. My military advisers had told me that each military division stationed in Poland or Hungary cost twice as much to maintain as the same division on Soviet territory.

Then, I understood. If our troops are stationed in some other country, that government receives a lot of additional income. Gomulka said, 'It's politics, after all, and you can't measure politics in quantitative expenditures.' This is true, but nevertheless it was we who were doing the spending.

Ibid., pp. 119–20.

DOCUMENT 6   CZECHOSLOVAKIA

Novotny expresses the nervousness of east European communist leaders who felt that the debunking of Stalin at the Twentieth Party Congress had weakened them. Czechoslovakia had had its own show trials but the Communist Party was aware of the dangers of resurrecting the past. When Novotny was replaced by Dubcek in early 1968 the political climate became much warmer, but this led to the tragic events of August 1968 when the Soviet Union and other Warsaw Pact countries invaded. Whereas previously there had been much goodwill towards Moscow, this now evaporated. Khrushchev was quite wrong about the true aspirations of the Czechs and Slovaks.

(i) We wanted to go easy on Stalin, even in death. We used to blame the devil, and say what had happened was the devil's work. First Yezhov, then Yagoda was the devil, later Beria.

There was no logic in this, because Beria came on the scene only after the meat grinder had done most of its work. Beria was mainly responsible for the cleanup that followed. He only continued the work that Stalin, aided by Yezhov and Yagoda, had started, if you can call the annihilation of human beings work.

I told Novotný there had been a great internal struggle over giving a report on Stalin's crimes to the congress. The main opponents of the idea were Molotov, Kaganovich, and Voroshilov, the same Voroshilov who was later given a hero's funeral and in whose honor a city was named. He was responsible for killing people in Voroshilovgrad [now Lugansk, in the Ukraine]. How many people died because of that man?

Soviet citizens must have the right to call things by their own names. We still haven't the courage for that. Crimes cannot be forgiven, especially crimes as heinous as those committed by Stalin and his closest aides, Molotov, Kaganovich, and Voroshilov. We must not forgive them. To do so would mean to give our blessing to new criminals for new crimes. In discussions with party representatives of all the other socialist countries, we said they also had to take a critical look and correct mistakes that had been made. We were completely sure that the cases there had been faked too, and that innocent people, honest Communists, loyal to the revolution, and loyal to the cause of Marxism-Leninism, had suffered. They had become the victims of ruthless excess.

When I expressed these ideas to Novotný, I was struck by his reaction. He seemed very nervous. He flinched and said, 'No Comrade Khrushchi' – that's what he called me, Comrade Khrushchi – 'no, that's not the way it was with us. We did everything according to the letter of the law. We had grounds for the arrests and the harsh sentences.'

'Comrade Novotný', I said, 'I don't want to argue with you. We're making this recommendation on the basis of our own experience. Like you, we believed everything was done according to the law, that all our arrests and executions were well grounded, that those convicted were truly enemies of the people. Now, after our lawyers have looked at the evidence, it seems that there was not nearly enough to arrest anyone in the first place.'

'No,' insisted Novotný, 'It was different with us. We –.

'Look', I said, 'you executed Slansky, the general secretary of the Czechoslovak Communist party.'

I remember all too well Stalin trying to persuade Gottwald that he also must have enemies of the people. Gottwald answered that they had no such enemies. I remember how quickly Stalin's Chekist advisers found the enemies of the people by using the methods of Beria and Yezhov. Those methods are easy to implement as soon as there is an order. Stalin issued the order. We should speak about Stalin's methods. ...

Ibid., pp. 134–6.

(ii) On the radio these days I often hear irresponsible statements about Czechoslovakia. Honestly, I don't understand how we could reach this state of affairs in our relations with Czechoslovakia. The situation is critical. Before this our relationship with the people was so warm, so open and honest. How could this have happened? I don't really understand it even today. I am firmly convinced that the Czech people are committed to building socialism, that they support the Communist Party of Czechoslovakia, and that they are our closest allies and most loyal partners in the struggle to build socialism.

I simply can't agree that the Czechs have succumbed to imperialist propaganda, that they want to change the course of their society and return to capitalist means of production. I don't believe it. I certainly don't want to believe it. It contradicts all my understanding of progressive Marxist-Leninist teachings.

Ibid., p. 139.

DOCUMENT 7   **BULGARIA**

Khrushchev had a low opinion of Bulgarians and this was held against him in October 1964. It is worth noting that Bulgaria, in the west, was held to be the most loyal among socialist states in eastern Europe to the Soviet Union.

There are other examples of how supporting cooperative relations with fraternal countries creates problems. The Soviet Union imports tomatoes from Bulgaria, but they are garbage. I can taste the poor quality when Nina Petrovna buys them. Why do I say they are lousy? I grew up eating Bulgarian tomatoes, and they were really something back then. The Bulgarians saw to it that they came to market fresh, but now we get something else, from a 'fraternal' country. The Bulgarians have gotten used to the fact that Russians will eat any old shit, if you'll excuse the expression. They pick the tomatoes when they're still hard and green, then store them. When they ship them to us, they turn ripe on the way. The result is garbage.

The Bulgarians also export tomatoes to West Germany, but what a difference in the fruit! I'm sure that the West Germans wouldn't buy the ones we get. Why? Because there's competition in that market, while we are compelled to buy from our fraternal Bulgarians. They've got nothing else with which to repay their debt to us. And who suffers? The consumer. The one who has to eat these tomatoes – that's who suffers.

The Bulgarians don't eat the tomatoes they send us – you won't find garbage like that in their markets. They eat tomatoes picked one day and sold the next morning. They have wonderful tomatoes right there. The Bulgarians are the best gardeners in the world, I know.

Ibid., pp. 111–12.

DOCUMENT 8   CHINA

Mao felt insulted when he visited Moscow for the first time as head of the People's Republic of China. He asked for substantial aid but was given only a modest loan, on which he was required to pay interest. When Stalin died Mao regarded himself as the doyen of the communist world and expected to be consulted on all major issues. Khrushchev had no intention of treating Mao in this fashion and wanted to demonstrate that the Soviet Union was dominant. The second extract is by Shmuel Mikunis, then leader of the Israeli Communist Party. It captures nicely Mao's vanity.

(i) 'If there is an attack on the Soviet Union, I would recommend that you not offer resistance.'

I was immediately on my guard: The imperialist states attack the Soviet Union, and we must not offer resistance? How could that be? What were we supposed to do?

Mao Zedong explained: 'Retreat for a year, or two or three. Force your enemy to stretch out his lines of communications. That will weaken him. Then, with our combined strength, we will go for the enemy together and smash him.'

I said, 'Comrade Mao, I don't know what to say. What you are saying is out of the question. Can you imagine us retreating for a year? Would the war go on for a year? Think about what can happen in a year!'

Mao answered, 'But in World War II you retreated to Stalingrad for two years. Why can't you retreat for three years now? If you retreat to the Urals, China is nearby. We'll use our resources and territory to help you smash the enemy.'

I said, 'Comrade Mao, we see things differently. We believe in immediate retaliation, with all the weapons at our disposal. Our ability to do that is what deters our enemy. We can keep him from committing aggression in the first place.'

'No,' said Mao, 'I don't think that's right.'

Later, I often wondered how to argue against such reasoning. Mao is a clever man. How could he think this way? Could it have been a provocation? I can't believe Mao would try something so stupid with us. Could he really have believed that what he was saying made military sense?

Ibid., pp. 147–50.

(ii) In the way he spoke and held himself, and in the way he replied to questions, [Mao Zedong] resembled a sage of ancient China. He gave me that impression, at any rate, when I saw him for the first time in St George's Hall. He had trouble with his legs and usually spoke sitting down. His favourite theme, to which he kept returning, was World War III. He regarded this as an absolutely inevitable event, for which one must be ready at any moment. I would even go so far as to say that he lived and thought in terms of this war, as though it had already begun. I well remember how he sat there, surrounded by Soviet delegates, and philosophized aloud: 'Nehru and I', he said, 'are at present discussing the question of how many people would perish in an atomic war. Nehru says that we'll lose a milliard and a half, but I say only a milliard and a quarter.'

Palmiro Togliatti then asked him: 'But what would become of Italy as a result of such a war?' Mao Tse-tung looked at him in a thoughtful way and replied, quite coolly: 'But who told you that Italy must survive? Three hundred million Chinese will be left, and that will be enough for the human race to continue.' Mao saw himself as the leader of world Communism, the direct successor of Stalin, and therefore assumed that he had the right to intervene in the affairs of all Communist Parties, including the Soviet Party. He talked a lot, but in an absolutely peremptory way: he did not so much talk as insist. ... For instance, he was very displeased at Khrushchev's having removed Molotov, Malenkov and Kaganovich from the leadership and said: 'You should have consulted me before you took that step.'
,

Vremya i My (Tel Aviv), no. 48. 1979, pp. 164–5.

DOCUMENT 9   **KHRUSHCHEV AND CULTURE**

There was always tension between Khrushchev and the creative intelligentsia. He was always grappling with two opposing views: that the artist was a soldier in the class war and that artists should be free to express themselves. It is significant that Mikhail Suslov, who can be described as Brezhnev's desiccated ideological calculating machine, warned against opening the sluice gates of criticism. He was acutely aware of the lack of legitimacy of the Soviet system and the dangers of open discussion and criticism. Ideologists always felt insecure.

That's talk for children. We have the most real – and I might even say the most cruel – censorship. We should not turn criticism into censorship. In such cases critics and ideologues turn into police bullies.

I feel proud and pleased of the way we dealt with Aleksandr Solzhenitsyn's *One Day in the Life of Ivan Denisovich*. We decided at the 'highest level' – on the fifth and sixth floors of the Central Committee, where the commissions convened.

It began when Comrade Tvardovsky arranged a meeting with me. He brought the work to me, briefed me on the contents, and gave me his opinion. Tvardovsky said, 'Comrade Khrushchev, I think this work is very good. From this work I can see that its author is going to become a great writer.' He thought this was his first work.

Tvardovsky said, 'The theme raised in the book may, of course, evoke a range of different attitudes both to the work and to the author. Please read it yourself and make your own judgment. I ask you not to interfere with its publication. I will publish it in my magazine.'

I did not know the biography of Solzhenitsyn. We knew from his work and reports I received that he had been in the camps for a long time – in Kolyma, probably. What he describes in his work is derived from his own experiences in the camps, and it is possible that he modelled the main character after himself.

I read the book. It is very heavy, but it was written well, in my opinion. The life of Ivan Denisovich and his surroundings are well described and deeply disturbing. This is the main quality required in a work of art. It evokes revulsion toward what existed in the camps and the conditions under which Ivan Denisovich and his friends lived while they served their terms in the camp. ...

At that time, almost all my comrades agreed with me. We had discussions, and there were some differences. Actually, only one voice, Suslov's, squawked in opposition. His words were like a policeman's. He wanted to hold everything in check. 'You cannot do this. That's all there is to it,' he said. He distrusted the people. 'How will the people perceive this? How will the people understand?' The people will understand correctly – that was my reply. The people will always distinguish good from bad.

Nikita Khrushchev [60], pp. 196–8.

DOCUMENT 10   SERGEI KHRUSHCHEV AND HIS FATHER

Sergei records that his father would discuss certain topics endlessly – agriculture, rockets, and so on – but in accepting the charlatan claims of T. D. Lysenko he had a closed mind. It was simply impossible to get through to him that Lysenko (who opposed genetics) was harming Soviet science.

What I couldn't understand was his stubborn unwillingness to hear the other side. I guess he just trusted his advisers, who were all in Lysenko's camp, while he thought we simply weren't qualified in this field. He supported the spirit of competition in other branches of science and technology. Engineers made their proposals and then entered into competition; it was the results themselves that defined whose was best. But on this issue, Father was adamant. His final, immovable argument was to accuse someone of 'idealism', to refer to the way bourgeois ideology had penetrated our society.

Sergei Khrushchev [62], p. 42.

DOCUMENT 11   THE TWENTIETH PARTY CONGRESS

This speech broke the tradition of Party infallibility and set in train events which eventually destroyed communist power. The speech shocked and stunned delegates. Many of them may have heard rumours of such things but had dismissed them as bourgeois propaganda. The speech devastated western Communist Parties and led to many resignations. Even more gory details were revealed in 1961. Nevertheless, all the revelations were selective. Only Glasnost and the end of the Soviet regime laid bare the true dimension of the crimes committed in the name of the Soviet Union and socialism.

Having at its disposal numerous data showing brutal wilfulness toward party cadres, the Central Committee has created a party commission under the control of the Central Committee Presidium; it was charged with investigating what made possible mass repressions against the majority of the Central Committee members and candidates elected at the 17th Congress of the All-Union Communist Party (Bolsheviks).

The commission has become acquainted with a large quantity of materials in the NKVD archives and with other documents and has established many facts pertaining to the fabrication of cases against Communists, to false accusations, to glaring abuses of socialist legality, which resulted in the death of innocent people. It became apparent that many party, Soviet and economic activists, who were branded in 1937–1938 as 'enemies', were actually never enemies, spies, wreckers, etc., but were always honest Communists; they were only so stigmatized and, often, no longer able to bear barbaric tortures, they charged themselves (at the order of the investigative judges – falsifiers) with all kinds of grave and unlikely crimes.

After the criminal murder of Sergei M. Kirov, mass repressions and brutal acts of violation of socialist legality began. On the evening of December 1, 1934, on Stalin's initiative (without the approval of the Political Bureau – which was passed two days later, casually), the Secretary of the Presidium of the Central Executive Committee, Yenukidze, signed the following directive:

1 Investigative agencies are directed to speed up the cases of those accused of the preparation or execution of acts of terror.
2 Judicial organs are directed not to hold up the execution of death sentences, pertaining to crimes of this category in order to consider the possibility of pardon, because the Presidium of the Central Executive Committee of the USSR does not consider as possible the receiving of petitions of this sort.
3 The organs of the Commissariat of Internal Affairs are directed to execute the death sentences against criminals of the above-mentioned category immediately after the passage of sentences.

This directive became the basis for mass acts of abuse against socialist legality. During many of the fabricated court cases, the accused were charged with 'the preparation' of terroristic acts; this deprived them of any possibility that their cases might be re-examined, even when they stated before the court that their 'confessions' were secured by force, and when, in a convincing manner, they disproved the accusations against them.

Let us also recall the 'affair of the doctor-plotters'. (Animation in the hall.) Actually there was no 'affair' outside of the declaration of the woman doctor Timashuk, who was probably influenced or ordered by someone (after all, she was an unofficial collaborator of the organs of state security) to write Stalin a letter in which she declared that doctors were applying supposedly improper methods of medical treatment.

Such a letter was sufficient for Stalin to reach an immediate conclusion that there are doctor-plotters in the Soviet Union. He issued orders to arrest a group of eminent Soviet medical specialists. He personally issued advice on the conduct of the investigation and the method of interrogation of the arrested persons. He said that the academican Vinogradov should be put in chains, another one should be beaten. Present at this Congress as a delegate is the former Minister of State Security, Comrade Ignatiev, Stalin told him curtly:

> If you do not obtain confessions from the doctors we will shorten you by a head. (Tumult in the hall.)

Stalin personally called the investigative judge, gave him instructions, advised him on which investigative methods should be used; these methods were simple – beat, beat and once again, beat.

Shortly after the doctors were arrested, we members of the Political Bureau received protocols with the doctors' confessions of guilt. After distributing these protocols, Stalin told us,

> You are blind like young kittens; what will happen without me? The country will perish because you do not know how to recognize enemies.

The case was so presented that no-one could verify the facts on which the investigation was based. There was no possibility of trying to verify facts by contacting those who had made the confessions of guilt.

N.S. Khrushchev [63], pp. 32–5, 62–3.

DOCUMENT 12   YUGOSLAVIA

Yugoslavia was a competitor in the race to communism, and there was always concern in Moscow lest better relations with Tito would make Yugoslav socialism too attractive to the east Europeans. Hence Tito was called on to acknowledge the leading role of the Soviet Union. The story recorded here is quite revealing and can be seen also as an implicit criticism of many Soviet deputies. The comment about the Soviet Union frightening itself is quite perceptive. Khrushchev appears to be conceding that all the accusations against Yugoslavia had no basis in fact and were necessitated by politics.

(i) I liked Tito. He had a lively personality, and he was a simple man. I liked Kardelj, too. When I first met Djilas, he impressed me with his quick and subtle wit. He struck me as a good man. I won't deny that I now have quite a different opinion of him, but that's beside the point. I remember that one evening between acts at the opera [in Kiev], Djilas told us a number of fables which he'd thought up himself. One in particular sticks in my mind, and I'd like to tell it here:

Once upon a time a dog, a cow, and an ass lived in a village somewhere in Yugoslavia. Things went from bad to worse there, and finally the dog, the cow, and the ass decided to run away into the mountains. They wandered around in the mountains for some time until they started to get hungry and homesick. They decided to send the dog back to town to see if the situation there had improved. Soon the dog came running back as fast as his legs would carry him. 'It's still too hard to live in the village,' he reported. 'They don't allow barking. How can a dog live if he's forbidden to bark?' So the three of them continued to wander through the mountains for a little while longer. Then they decided to send the cow to reconnoiter. 'Since you don't bark,' said the dog and the ass to the cow, 'it won't bother you that they don't allow barking.' So off the cow went. Some time passed, and the cow returned, obviously in great distress. 'It's impossible,' she said, 'simply impossible, I tell you! As soon as I arrived in town people started attacking me. They grabbed me by the nipples and started sucking and tugging! I kept bolting away, and they almost tore my nipples off! I just barely escaped!' So they continued to live in the mountains. Finally they decided to try one last time, and the ass agreed to go down to the village. A short time passed, and the ass came running back as fast as his legs would carry him. 'It's impossible, absolutely impossible to live in town!' he cried. 'Why?' the others asked. 'What happened?' 'Well,' said the ass, 'as soon as I arrived in town they tried to put me up for office. They were having their elections, and they wanted to elect me to parliament. I barely got away!'

Tito looked at Djilas sternly and said 'Are you trying to tell us by your fable that we elect asses to parliament?' But Tito was just joking. He laughed, Djilas laughed, and we all laughed.

Nikita Khrushchev [57], pp. 340–1.

(ii) After Stalin died, we began to exchange opinions in our leadership about the possibility of re-establishing contact with the Yugoslavs and liquidating the hostility which had been created by Stalin between the Soviet Union and Yugoslavia. This idea ran into sharp opposition from the outset. How could we restore relations with the Yugoslavs, people argued, when they had already slipped back into capitalism? Their economy had been swallowed up by American monopolistic capital; private property had been reinstated; private banks had been set up. Mikhail Suslov was particularly adamant in resisting the idea of trying to relieve the tension between us and the Yugoslavs. He insisted that Yugoslavia was no longer a Socialist country.

I think the reason for all these ridiculous claims was that we had been so estranged from the Yugoslavs and we had thought up so many accusations against them that we'd started to believe what we'd been telling ourselves. It's like in that old story about the mullah [a Muhammadan religious teacher] who is walking through the village square telling people that back where he's just come from they're giving away free lamb and rice. Word quickly spreads through the town, and everyone starts running in the direction where he pointed. When the mullah sees everyone running, he stops somebody and asks, 'What's happening?' 'They're giving away free lamb and rice over there!' So the mullah hikes up his skirts and runs along with the crowd to get free food, even though he made the whole story up himself. It was just the same with Yugoslavia. We'd made up a story about all the terrible things the Yugoslavs were doing, and we'd heard the story so often that we started to believe it ourselves.

Ibid., pp. 342–3.

DOCUMENT 13   **THE GENEVA SUMMIT OF 1955**

The Soviet Union's inferiority complex surfaces here. The Swiss were quite determined that Bulganin, the Prime Minister, would be accorded full honours while Khrushchev, as First Party Secretary, held no governmental post. Khrushchev is agreeably surprised with his welcome in East Berlin, only two years after the uprising.

There was a ceremony in honor of the four delegations at the airport, a military parade followed by an invitation for the head of each delegation to review the troops. An unpleasant incident occurred during this ceremony. Bulganin, as the head of our delegation, was supposed to step forward after the parade and inspect the honor guard. Just before he did so, a Swiss protocol officer suddenly stepped right in front of me and stood with his back up against my nose. My first impulse was to shove him out of the way. Later I realized he had done this on the instruction of the Swiss government. He had been told to make sure that I couldn't step forward with Bulganin to review the troops. I wasn't permitted to join that part of the ceremony, so the Swiss government very rudely had that man stand in front of me!

As we drove off to our residences, I noticed that Eisenhower's bodyguards had to run along behind his car. This struck us as being extremely odd. For a man to keep up with a moving car is no mean trick, nor is it easy for a car to pace itself to a man on foot. Four years later I saw the same thing again when Eisenhower met me at the airport in Washington at the beginning of my visit to America. Once again, there were those hearty fellows from his personal bodyguard running along behind the car in which he drove me back into the city.

We stopped off in East Berlin on the way back to our Homeland, and there we joined the leaders of the German Democratic Republic and issued another joint statement. We were greeted with full honors in East Berlin. Huge crowds of people came out to cheer us. I had been to Germany before, but this was the first time I had been there in an official capacity. I expected there to be some displays of hostility toward us, but there were none. There were a few sour faces, but not many. In the main we were welcomed enthusiastically. Our warm reception in Berlin reinforced our conviction that the Germans were fed up with making war, and that now they wanted to build strong, friendly relations with us.

Ibid., pp. 358–9, 363.

DOCUMENT 14   **GREAT BRITAIN**

The visit of Khrushchev and Bulganin to Britain in April 1956 aroused enormous interest as it was the first Soviet official visit to a Western country. Sir Anthony Eden (later Lord Avon) was Prime Minister and Selwyn Lloyd foreign secretary. Is the little bird story infantile or is it more profound? Gorky Street (now Tverskaya Street) is a major thoroughfare in Moscow. The Russians were keen to engage in one-up-manship with their new plane. Khrushchev is very frank about Soviet procurement practices, but is confident enough to concede that they were conned from time to time.

(i) After we were settled, we began discussions with the British government leaders. Their side was led by Eden and Lloyd. I think Macmillan also took part in these negotiations. Substantively our talks didn't add much to what had come out of our Geneva meeting. The main issues were still Germany, disarmament, and peaceful coexistence. We had already seen that the West wasn't yet ready to deal seriously with these very important issues. The Western powers were still trying to coax us into an accommodation on their terms.

I remember one incident that captures the atmosphere of our talks in London. Bulganin, Lloyd, and I were riding in the same car on our way to visit some educational institution. Lloyd was very proper and friendly. At one point he turned to me and said, 'You know, a little birdie perched on my shoulder the other day and chirped into my ear that you are selling arms to Yemen.'

I said, 'Well, apparently there are all sorts of little birds flying about these days, chirping all kinds of different things, because one perched on my shoulder, too, and told me that you're selling arms to Egypt and Iraq. This little birdie told me that you'll try to sell arms to anyone who will buy them from you and sometimes even to people who don't want to buy them from you.'

'I guess it's true: there are all sorts of birdies. Some of them are chirping in your ear, and some in ours.'

'Yes,' I said, 'but wouldn't it be nice if all the little birdies started chirping the same thing in both of our ears – that we should assume a mutually binding obligation not to sell arms to anyone? Then wouldn't all the birdies be making a contribution to the common cause of peace?'

Ibid., pp. 366–7.

(ii) Eden invited Bulganin and me to spend the night at Chequers. We were shown to separate rooms upstairs. In the morning I woke up early and went out into the hall, looking for Bulganin's room so I could wake him up. I knocked on a door, thinking it was Bulganin's. A woman's voice rang out, she was obviously surprised and frightened. I realized that I had almost walked in on Eden's wife. I turned around then hurried back to my room without apologizing or identifying myself. Bulganin and I had a good laugh over the incident, but we decided not to mention it to our hosts.

The next day we had an appointment to visit with Queen Elizabeth. We didn't have to wear any special sort of clothes. We had told Eden in advance that if the Queen didn't mind receiving us in our everyday business suits, it was fine. If she did object, then it was just too bad. We had some preconceived notions about this kind of ceremony, and we weren't going to go out of our way to get all dressed up in tails and top hats or anything else that they might have insisted on for an audience with the Queen. I remember once in Moscow we were watching a documentary film which showed Anastas Ivanovich Mikoyan all decked out as our official emissary in Pakistan. We all roared with laughter at the sight of him. He really did look like an old-fashioned European gentleman. I might mention that the fancy airs required of ambassadors by foreign diplomats were not alien to Anastas Ivanovich.

Anyway, we arrived at the Queen's palace on a warm, pleasant day. According to Eden, April is the best time of year, with the least rain. There were throngs of tourists sight-seeing on the palace grounds. Eden told us that we would find the Queen to be a simple, but very bright and very pleasant woman. She met us as we came in to the palace. She had her husband and two of her children with her. We were introduced. She was dressed in a plain, white dress. She looked like the sort of young woman you'd be likely to meet walking along Gorky Street on a balmy summer afternoon.

She gave us a guided tour around the palace and then invited us to have a glass of tea with her. We sat around over tea and talked about one thing and another.

The Queen was particularly interested in our plane, the Tu-104, which flew our mail to us while we were in England. Actually, part of the reason we had the Tu-104 fly to London while we were there was to show the English that we had a good jet passenger plane. This was one of the first jet passenger planes in the world, and we wanted our hosts to know about it.

Ibid., pp. 368–9.

(iii) I remember when I was in England [1956] Academician Kurchatov accompanied us. A British scientist received Kurchatov and took him to visit various scientific and research institutes. We were then obliged to extend an invitation to this British scientist to visit our country. To show this British scientist something of ours in return was exceedingly difficult for us. We had been inculcated for decades with the belief that the imperialists were our sworn enemies. They would spy on and sneak a look at everything of ours and not show us anything of theirs. They would recruit our people and worm their way in. To a great extent this was true, of course, but we cannot take such an absurdity to the extreme of scaring even ourselves and losing all faith in our own people. We must not lose sight of the fact that our people were fighting to build socialism, that they had their own integrity and national pride, their own worth. All these feelings had been smothered within us. For Stalin such emotions did not exist at all. With us, only police measures existed, to restrain and not let go. To put our international scientific relations in simple words: 'You can't take a step toward me, and I am forbidden to take a step toward you.'

And so we had only one choice: to steal – though, of course, you have to be smart enough to do that. True, everyone steals. All countries steal, even if they can buy licences and obtain what they need legally. Given the chance, they steal instead. I do not say this to condemn this method of contact. I feel that it is better, of course, to maintain contacts on a basis of licensing exchanges and payments for obtaining them. This is so much more simple and beneficial than theft. When you buy stolen property you don't always get exactly what you need, and a thief sometimes is a stooge. Sometimes what he thinks he is stealing has actually been sold to him by order of an intelligence agency. I know of one such case myself.

When Grechko commanded our troops in East Germany [1957–60], we purchased an American missile from West Germany. When it had been delivered to our researchers for analysis they began to laugh. What had happened? The agent who sold it probably became suspicious and realized that the man he was dealing with was a Soviet intelligence officer. He palmed off an inferior missile on our man to humiliate us with a piece of junk.

Nikita Khrushchev [60], pp. 194–5.

DOCUMENT 15   THE ERECTION OF THE BERLIN WALL

Khrushchev admits that the Wall was a symbol of weakness, but he must have realised that it could not stand for ever. When the Wall fell on 9 November 1989 it signalled the demise of the GDR.

By 1961 an unstable situation had been created in the GDR. At the time, there was an economic boom in West Germany. West Germany needed workers badly and lured them from Italy, Spain, Turkey, Yugoslavia, and other countries. Numbers of the intelligentsia, students and people with higher education, left the GDR because West Germany paid office workers more than they were paid in the GDR and other socialist countries. The question of whether this or that system is progressive ought to be decided in political terms. However, many people decide it in the pit of their stomach. They don't consider tomorrow's gains but only today's income – and today West German industry pays you more.

Walter Ulbricht even asked us to help by providing a labor force. This was a difficult issue to face. We didn't want to give them unskilled workers. Why? Because we didn't want our workers to clean their toilets. I had to tell Comrade Ulbricht: 'Imagine how a Soviet worker would feel. He won the war and now he has to clean your toilets. It will not only be humiliating – it will produce an explosive reaction in our people. We cannot do this. Find a way out yourself.'

What could he do? He had to appeal for stronger discipline; but they still kept on running away because qualified workers could find better conditions in West Germany.

I spoke to Pervukhin, our ambassador in Germany, about the establishment of border control. He gave me a map of West Berlin. The map was very poor. I asked Pervukhin to share the idea with Ulbricht and also to ask Marshal Yakubovsky to send me a new map. Yakubovsky was the commander in Berlin who developed the actual plan. We discussed the idea and the map that Yakubovsky had drawn.

Ulbricht beamed with pleasure. 'This is the solution! This will help. I am for this.'

I told Pervukhin, 'Tell nobody about this. Keep it a secret.'

Unanimously, we decided to execute the plan as soon as possible. We called a closed meeting, with party secretaries and members of the Council of Ministers attending.

Ibid., pp. 168–9.

DOCUMENT 16   SAKHAROV AND NUCLEAR TESTING

Academician Andrei Sakharov, the father of the Soviet atomic bomb, warns Khrushchev of the consequences of resuming nuclear testing. In reply, Khrushchev is very frank about the need to show strength in international affairs in order to warn the West against attempting to dismantle the Berlin Wall.

I recall the summer of 1961, when a meeting had been arranged between Khrushchev, the Chairman of the Council of Ministers, and a number of atomic scientists. We were told that we had to prepare for a new series of tests, which were to provide support for the USSR's policy on the German question (the Berlin Wall). I wrote a note to Khrushchev, saying: 'The revival of these tests after the three-year moratorium will be a breach of the test-ban treaty and will check the move towards disarmament: it will lead to a fresh round in the arms race, especially in the sphere of inter-continental missiles and anti-missile defence.' I had this note passed along the rows of seats until it reached him. He put it in his breast pocket and invited all those present to dine with him. As we sat around the table, he made an impromptu speech, which I found memorable because of its frankness; in it he gave expression to something more than merely his own opinion. This, more or less, is what he said: 'Sakharov is a good scientist, but he should leave foreign policy to those of us who are specialists in this subtle art. Strength alone can throw our enemy into confusion. We cannot say out loud that we base our policy on strength, but that is how it has to be. I would be a ditherer and not the Chairman of the Council of Ministers if I were to listen to people like Sakharov.'

A.D. Sakharov, *O Strane i mire*, Khronika, New York, 1976, pp. vii–viii.

DOCUMENT 17   THE CUBAN MISSILE CRISIS

The crisis brought the world to the brink of nuclear war. Cuba had to be defended against another American attempt to invade, but the Soviet Union did not have enough intercontinental ballistic missiles to provide a nuclear umbrella for the island. Intermediate-range missiles placed in Cuba might solve the problem. During the crisis Khrushchev insisted that the missiles were defensive, but he here reveals that they were targeted on US cities in order to inflict maximum damage. He made contact with President Kennedy by letter, and vice versa. After the crisis a telephone hot line between the White House and the Kremlin was established.

I was haunted by the knowledge that the Americans could not stomach having Castro's Cuba right next door to them. Sooner or later the US would do something. It had the strength and it had the means ... How were we supposed to strengthen and reinforce Cuba? With diplomatic notes and TASS statements? The idea arose of placing our missile units in Cuba ... We concluded that we could send 42 missiles, each with a warhead of one megatonne. We picked targets in the US to inflict the maximum damage. We saw that our weapons could inspire terror. The two nuclear weapons the US used against Japan at the end of the war were toys by comparison.

Time, 1 Oct. 1990, pp. 76–7.

DOCUMENT 18   AN AMBASSADOR'S RECOLLECTIONS

Sir Frank Roberts, a British diplomat who enjoyed a glittering career, reflects on Khrushchev. He could not resist threatening to use his nuclear missiles against Britain but calmed down when answered in kind. Roberts also reveals Khrushchev's great love of the Russian classics and his perceptive comments on Germans and Germany.

Khrushchev's long absence from Moscow had another important effect. Being out of sight he was also safely out of mind as a potential successor to Stalin in the immediate post-war years. When I was first in Moscow in 1939 and later in 1941, at Yalta in February 1945 and immediately after that Minister in Moscow until the autumn of 1947 or again in Moscow as British representative in the Berlin blockade negotiations in the summer of 1948, I do not recall seeing Khrushchev at any of the many Kremlin dinners and receptions hosted by Stalin and attended by other members of the Politburo. Zhdanov on the one hand, and the strange double act of Malenkov and Beria on the other, appeared to be the main contenders for the succession until Zhdanov's death in 1948. Nor do I recall ever hearing Khrushchev's name so much as mentioned in this context. So his rise to supreme power in the two years after Stalin's death at the expense of better-educated and apparently better-equipped rivals came as a surprise and had much in common with Stalin's own rise to the top after Lenin's death. Behind his bluff and genial manner he was a good organiser and a cunning intriguer with strong roots in the Communist Party institutions which, unlike Malenkov then and Kosygin later, he regarded as the true source of political power. With all his innovations and brainwaves, he always regarded himself first and foremost as a loyal Party man. ...

So it was to a very different and more agreeable Moscow life that I returned in 1960, as compared with that I had experienced under Stalin in the 1940s. Delegation after delegation of British and other Western 'experts' in all fields, including nuclear and other scientists, doctors and businessmen, came to Moscow, each such visit providing contacts with their Soviet opposite numbers who poured into the British and other embassies to a gratifying if at times embarrassing degree.

Khrushchev set the tone himself by attending parties and receptions continually, whether as host or guest, dragging his colleagues along with him like a *corps de ballet* behind the prima ballerina. On these occasions he singled out Western Ambassadors and foreign non-communists for special attention. He was also readily available for more serious discussions in his Kremlin office with diplomats and well-known foreign ministers in Moscow saw much more of him than would be seen by diplomats of a Western head of government. These meetings were never dull, although they could on occasions be stormy. I will recall some of them to give the flavour of the man.

At one Kremlin reception I had been warned beforehand that he had just made a speech elsewhere rather insulting to the British and I intended to be very cold with him. He at once singled me out and in full view of the assembled guests was demonstratively friendly, saying that he often said things he should not and his remarks should not always be taken too seriously, going on to give me a bear-hug when I had asked him in the course of a long conversation whether bears were still to be found in central Russia and ending with several toasts in brandy, which he was at that time under strict doctor's orders not to drink. On another occasion I had arrived at his office with a message from Harold Macmillan, which I said I would just leave with him to consider and return later for his reply. He insisted, however, that I must stay, because no one ever saw him for less than an hour. If I left at once his staff would think our countries were going to war. He would not, however, even open the envelope until after I had left and meanwhile we might have a general conversation, for example on books we had each been reading. It emerged that he was in the middle of *War and Peace*, which he tried to reread every year and from which he quoted long passages, as I afterwards checked, with great accuracy. When it was my turn and I mentioned Turgenev's *Sportsman's Sketches*, he at once showed his familiarity with it. I have rarely passed a more surprising or a more agreeable hour.

But these meetings could be less agreeable. Just before the building of the Berlin Wall in 1961 (of which we in Moscow had no advance warning) he took me aside at a reception to inform me that a certain General who had 'put down the Budapest rising' in 1956 had been appointed to command the Soviet troops around Berlin. When I failed to react with what he considered appropriate concern, he suddenly warned me that he could destroy Britain with eight nuclear bombs. But when I retorted that while six should be enough for a relatively small island, twenty of his major cities could then be destroyed by British nuclear weapons, he calmed down and again sent for drinks with which to toast each other. Another occasion in 1961, before the Berlin Wall, at the opening performance of our Royal Ballet at the Bolshoi Theatre, my wife and I were sent for to sup with him and several of his colleagues, not to talk about Margot Fonteyn and our dancers (who were not invited to this supper) but to impress upon me the importance of finding a solution to the crisis he had himself created over Berlin; he could not tolerate this bone in his throat any longer, but was offering us a way out in the substitution of a United Nations presence for that of the three Western powers.

I recall above all my farewell talk with Khrushchev just after he had climbed down in the Cuba Missile Crisis of 1962. I knew he was exhausted and expected that for once my time with him would be short. Exhausted he certainly was, but as he talked his batteries were recharged and he kept me for two hours to talk about Germany, which was to be my next post. He himself was then hoping to visit West Germany for the first time, having of course visited East Germany many times. There were none of the usual attacks upon German militarism and revanchism, but instead a most objective review of German virtues and failings, with the emphasis upon the virtues and upon how much Russians had learnt from Germans in the past.

McCauley [76], pp. 216–17, 221–22.

DOCUMENT 19   **THE INDICTMENT**

The fifteen-point indictment is devastating.

1   His work in his capacity as leader of the Party and the Government had been marred by grave mistakes. He had taken hasty and ill-considered decisions and had encouraged the wanton proliferation of administrative bodies and hierarchical levels. In the preceding two or three years he had concentrated a great deal of power in his own hands and had begun to abuse it. He had taken credit personally for all the country's achievements and successes, had flouted the authority of the Presidium by slighting its members, treating them

with contempt and refusing to listen to their views and had lectured them and everyone else unceasingly. Despite frequent appeals from members of the Presidium, he had ignored all critical comment.

2 The Soviet press had taken to publishing more and more about Khrushchev and his virtues. In 1963 the national newspapers had printed 120 photographs of him, and during the first nine months of 1964 140 had appeared in print. By contrast, photographs of Stalin had appeared in the press no more than ten or fifteen times a year. Khrushchev had surrounded himself with relations and journalists, furthermore, whose advice had evidently been more valuable to him than that of members of the Presidium, which had been obliged to rubber-stamp measures promoted by these people. The former leader had relied on the sycophancy of the press and the broadcasting services to bolster his self-esteem.

3 The Central Committee had removed the ex-premier's son-in-law, Adzhubei, from his job as editor-in-chief of *Izvestiya* because he was obsequious, incompetent and irresponsible. He had assumed the role of shadow Foreign Minister and had attempted to meddle in diplomatic matters at the highest level, confusing the ambassadors. On one occasion Adzhubei had spoken slightingly of Walter Ulbricht when on a visit to West Germany, and it had taken a great deal of tact to soothe the Democratic Republic afterwards.

4 The division of the obkoms into two parallel organizations, one industrial and the other agricultural, had caused a great deal of administrative confusion and had contributed to the formation of twin parties – a workers' party and a peasants' party.

5 Khrushchev had proposed the substitution of political departments in place of existing units of agricultural administration. His memorandum outlining the responsibilities of these new, specialized departments with respect to stockbreeding and the cultivation of crops had been called in by the Presidium in view of its manifest impracticality.

6 The ex-premier had considered himself a specialist in every sphere – agriculture, diplomacy, science, art – and had hectored everyone who crossed his path. In the German Democratic Republic, for example, he had not hesitated to instruct farmers in how to run their farms and had generally behaved as though he were in one of the Republics of the Soviet Union. Furthermore, many of the documents that had been prepared by the Central Committee had carried Khrushchev's name, as though he were to be credited with the wisdom of their conclusions.

7 Khrushchev had made impossible demands on the members of the Presidium: he had given them only forty-five minutes to respond to his memoranda – in writing. As a result, all consultation had been reduced to a formality, and meetings of the Presidium had become empty gestures.

8 Under Khrushchev the management of industry had become so complicated that the administrative hierarchy – the state committees, the economic councils, the Supreme Economic Council – was now unwieldy and inefficient, as was industry itself, which was less productive than it had been under former systems of management.

9 Khrushchev had devised and implemented policies that undermined the well-being of the workers. Rises in the price of meat, dairy products and certain manufactured goods had adversely affected living standards, and the supply of meat on the market had steadily diminished as a result of the general application of wholly fallacious theories about animal husbandry that had led to the slaughter of countless heads of cattle.

10 In interviews the ex-premier had lacked circumspection. He had done nothing to ameliorate the Soviet Union's relations with the People's Republic of China, for example. On one occasion he had remarked to some Japanese Members of Parliament that if the opinion of the Kazakhs in Sinkiang were to be canvassed, and if they declared a preference for Soviet rather than Chinese dominion, then the USSR would be obliged to annex the territory; on another he referred to Mao Tse-tung as 'an old galosh', and Mao had not been gratified by the description when it reached his ears. Khrushchev's treatment of Albania had also been less than sensitive.

11 Even friends of the Soviet Union had not escaped Khrushchev's censure. At a dinner held after one of the Comecon meetings Khrushchev had flung at Zhivkov, the Bulgarian premier, the remark that the Bulgars had always been parasites. The presence of dozens of representatives of socialist states and Communist Parties had inhibited Zhivkov, who had preserved a diplomatic silence. Khrushchev's comment testified to arrogance that was inappropriate in the leader of one of the world's great powers.

12 Khrushchev's attitude towards foreign trading partners had been cavalier. Poland, Romania and Finland had suffered particularly from his arbitrary changes of mind. In Poland a factory had been constructed in which AN-2 aeroplanes were to be produced. The Soviet Union had undertaken to purchase 500 of these from Poland. In the event the order was cancelled because the ex-premier had decided that the aircraft could be built more cheaply in the USSR. The decision amounted to a betrayal of Poland's trust and that of the 15,000 workers who were employed at the factory. Romania's loyalty had been tested by the Soviet Union's requirement that her oil be channelled directly into the Druzhba ('Friendship') pipeline at a time when Romania was delighted to be earning foreign currency through the sale of her oil. From Finland the USSR had ordered prefabricated cottages. Their manufacture had required the construction of a special factory, which lay idle when the order was withdrawn at the insistence of Khrushchev. As a consequence,

Finland had refused to invest in new plant when the Soviet Union later wished to place an order for new ships with Finnish shipyards. Furthermore, Khrushchev had resolutely ignored the Soviet Minister of Foreign Trade: during all his years in power he had neither received Patolichev nor even telephoned him.

13 The question of the Timiryazev Agricultural Academy: Khrushchev's decision to move the Academy to a remote spot in the depths of the country when he learned that it employed scientists who disagreed with his agricultural policies, ('They are wasting their time tilling the asphalt,' he said, in defence of his decision) had angered the members of the Presidium. By setting up commissions of various kinds, Khrushchev's colleagues had managed to delay the exile of the Academy, which had been established in Moscow a hundred years before – in short, they had sabotaged his instructions. When Khrushchev discovered one day that the Academy was still in Moscow he issued an order that it was to accept no more students. As the student body had shrunk, more and more teachers had been obliged to leave the Academy.

14 The ex-premier had mounted a wholly unjustifiable campaign against fallows and the private plots of collective farmers, who had had to battle against the weeds that grew vigorously on the land that had been confiscated but left uncultivated. He had defended Lysenko's nonsense in the face of vociferous protest from prominent scientists and had even proposed that the Soviet Academy of Sciences create two vacancies for friends of Lysenko. When Sakharov had challenged their candidature, he had been abused by Lysenko, who resented bitterly the rejection of his protégés and took up the matter with Khrushchev. The dissolution of the Academy itself was threatened. When Kosygin had shown some interest in the cultivation of grain in Kazakhstan Khrushchev had regarded this as interference in a sphere over which he himself had a monopoly. In a number of oblasts he had advocated the replacement of collective farms by state farms, although the latter were clearly less profitable.

15 In the promises that he had made to other nations, in his relations with foreign countries generally, Khrushchev had been indiscriminate and profligate. He had conferred on Nasser and Amer honours that were inappropriate; he had committed the Soviet Union to helping Iraq to construct a railway line 600 kilometres long at a time when the USSR herself was able to extend her own railway system by only just that much each year; he had seen fit to order Soviet engineers to build a stadium in Indonesia, where extreme poverty was endemic; he had taken his entire family with him when he toured Scandinavia, prompting the Western press to dub the visit a 'family picnic'.

Roy A. Medvedev [81], pp. 237–44.

DOCUMENT 20   NEIZVESTNY'S SCULPTURE

Neizvestny respected Khrushchev for many of his achievements while disagreeing fundamentally with him on others. The sculptor catches nicely some of the contradictions in Nikita Sergeevich's character.

'In a philosophical sense, life itself is based on antagonism between two principles,' Neizvestny declared in his usual way. 'One is bright, progressive, dynamic; the other is dark, reactionary, static. One strains to move forward, the other pulls back. This basic idea fits Nikita Sergeyevich's image quite well. He began to lead our country out of the darkness, and he exposed Stalin's crimes. The dawn broke for all of us, heralding the imminent rise of the sun. The light began to dispel the darkness.'

This approach helps us to understand the basic ideas reflected in the tombstone. The main component is white marble, its dynamic form bearing down on black granite. The darkness resists, struggles, refuses to yield – as with man himself. It's no accident that the head is on a white pedestal, or that the background remains dark. In the upper corner of the white is a symbolic representation of the sun. Rays extend down from it, dispelling the darkness. The head, the color of old gold on white, not only pleases the eye, it's also a symbol: the Romans immortalized their heroes this way. It all rests on the sturdy foundation of a bronze slab. It can't be budged. There's no reversing the process that's begun.

On the left of the slab, seen from the stele, there's a heart-shaped aperture. Red flowers ought to grow there, to symbolize enthusiasm and self-sacrifice.

Then there are the letters: on one side KHRUSHCHEV NIKITA SERGEYEVICH, and on the other the dates of birth and death. Nothing else, no explanation of any kind. It all has to be laconic, majestic.

Sergei Khrushchev [62], pp. 380–1.

CHRONOLOGY

1894   Nikita Sergeevich Khrushchev born in Kalinovka, Kursk guberniya, Russia.

1909   Moves to Yuzovka (now Donetsk).

1912   One of strike leaders at Bosse concern and sacked.

1914   Marries but wife dies of typhus in 1921.

1917   Becomes Bolshevik.

1918   Joins Party and fights in civil war.

1924   Marries Nina Petrovna Kukharchuk.
          Leaves Workers' Faculty without a diploma.

1925   Becomes first secretary of Petrovsko-Mariinsk *raion*, Yuzovka; attends Fourteenth Party Congress in Moscow as a non-voting delegate.

1927   Attends the Fifteenth Party Congress in Moscow as a full delegate.

1928   Becomes deputy to N.N. Demchenko, head of cadres selection, Kharkov.

1929   Moves to Kiev with Demchenko and later to Moscow to enter the Industrial Academy.

1931   Elected first secretary, Bauman raikom, Moscow, then first secretary, Krasnaya Presnya raikom, Moscow.

1934   Elected member of Central Committee at Seventeenth Party Congress, then first secretary, Moscow gorkom and second secretary, Moscow obkom.

1935   Elected first secretary, Moscow gorkom.

1938   Elected to Presidium, USSR Supreme Soviet, then candidate member of the Party Politburo, then first secretary, Communist Party of Ukraine.

1941   After German invasion becomes member of various military councils which makes him political commissar, promoted later to lieutenant-general.

1943   Re-enters burning Kiev and begins reconstruction.

1944   Elected Prime Minister of Ukraine and retains his position as Party leader.

1947 Dismissed as first Party secretary of Ukraine but remains Prime Minister; reinstated as party leader at end of year but loses post of Prime Minister.

1949 Moves to capital as first secretary, Moscow obkom and also elected a secretary of the Central Committee (CC).

1953 Stalin dies; Khrushchev removed as first secretary, Moscow gorkom, but becomes head of CC Secretariat when Malenkov chooses to be Prime Minister; arrest of Beria opens way for straight contest between Khrushchev and Malenkov for primacy; elected first secretary, CC, CPSU.

1954 Launches virgin lands programme; visits China.

1955 Visits Yugoslavia; Austrian Peace Treaty signed; Geneva summit of wartime Big Four; diplomatic relations with West Germany established; travels to Burma, India and Afghanistan.

1956 Visits England; secret speech at Twentieth Party Congress; upheavals in Poland and revolution in Hungary; Tito visits Soviet Union.

1957 Anti-Party group defeated; Khrushchev becomes strong, national leader; *de facto* Prime Minister as Bulganin had sided with defeated opponents; Sputnik launched; conference of ruling Communist and Workers' Parties, and non-ruling parties; gulf between Khrushchev and Mao widens; dismisses Marshal Zhukov as minister of defence; Pasternak's *Doctor Zhivago* published abroad.

1958 Becomes Prime Minister; Pasternak wins Nobel Prize; conflict with Yugoslavia intensifies; relations with China deteriorate; Berlin crisis begins.

1959 Twenty-first Party Congress launches Seven Year Plan; American exhibition at Sokolniki Park, Moscow, and famous exchanges with Nixon; visits US, then China, but visit not a success.

1960 Visits India, Burma, Indonesia, Afghanistan, France; Paris summit wrecked by U2 incident; attends UN Assembly and performs famous shoe-banging act; Sino–Soviet split evident.

1961 First manned flight in space; meets Kennedy in Vienna; erection of Berlin Wall; Twenty-second Party Congress launches race to communism.

1962 Cuban missile crisis; confrontation with Neizvestny at Manège; bifurcation of Party and governmental apparatus.

1963 Many agricultural reforms; poor harvest.

1964   Visits Poland and falls out with Mazurov; visits Egypt and confers on Nasser and Amer title of Hero of the Soviet Union; plot against him launched; dismissed as Party and government leader and commander-in-chief of Soviet armed forces; only Mikoyan stays loyal.

1966   Begins dictating memoirs.

1971   First volume of memoirs appears; dies of heart failure.

1974   Second volume of memoirs published.

1975   Monument by Neizvestny erected.

GLOSSARY

cadre Communist Party functionary.

Central Committee (CC) According to the Party statutes was the leading Party body; directed activities of Party between congresses, selected and appointed leading officials, directed the work of government bodies and public organisations through Party groups within them; each republic had its own CC; in reality Presidium was leading body.

CPSU Communist Party of the Soviet Union; in 1917 also called Bolshevik Party.

dacha Holiday home (sometimes very modest cottage or can be grand house) outside city.

gorkom Communist Party committee which ran a town or city.

Gulag Abbreviation for State Administration of Camps; name of prison system under Stalin.

KGB Committee of State Security or political police.

Komsomol Young Communist League.

krai Subdivision of republic; is an *oblast* which contains autonomous district.

kraikom Party committee which ran a *krai*.

Machine Tractor Stations Set up in early 1930s to maximise use of available machinery; disbanded 1958.

MGB Ministry of State Security or secret police; name used between 1946–53; thereafter KGB.

MVD Ministry of Internal Affairs; responsible for ordinary police (militia); merged with MGB under Beria in 1953.

NKVD People's Commissariat of Internal Affairs: responsible for police 1934–46 when commissariats were renamed ministries.

nomenklatura List of most important posts in state; and list of communists suitable for such posts.

obkom Party committee which ran an *oblast*.

oblast Subdivision of republic.

Politburo Political bureau; or key Party decision-making body.

Presidium of USSR Supreme Soviet: top policy-making body or executive
   committee: chairman of this body was head of state; of USSR Council of
   Ministers: approximated a government cabinet; of CC, CPSU: name of
   Politburo 1952–66.

raikom Party committee which ran a *raion*.

raion Subdivision of *oblast*, *krai* or city.

Secretariat of the CC Secretaries were responsible for the entire Party
   apparat; there was a first secretary, a second secretary and so on; often
   also members of the Politburo.

soviet Council: basic unit of local government.

sovnarkhozy Councils of the National Economy; responsible for a
   particular region; there were 105 in 1957, 47 in 1963 and none since
   1965.

USSR Supreme Soviet Highest organ of government; pretended to be
   parliament until 1989 when it became one; republics and autonomous
   republics also have Supreme Soviets.

vozhd Boss.

BIBLIOGRAPHY

1   Aksyutin, Yu. V., *Nikita Sergeevich Khrushchev: Materialy k biografii*, Izdatelstvo Politicheskoi Literatury, Moscow, 1989.
2   Aksyutin, Yu. V. and Volobuev, O.V., *XX Sezd: Novatsii i Dogmy*, Izdatelstvo Politicheskoi Literatury, Moscow, 1991.
3   Azrael, Jeremy R., *Managerial Power and Soviet Politics*, Harvard University Press, Cambridge, MA, 1966.
4   Belotserkovsky, Vadim, 'Workers' Struggles in the USSR in the Early Sixties', *Critique*, no. 10/11, 1979.
5   Bialer, Seweryn, *Stalin's Successors: Leadership, Stability and Change in the Soviet Union*, Cambridge University Press, Cambridge, 1980.
6   Blyakhman, L.S., Zdravomyslov, A.G. and Shkaratan, O.I., *Dvizhenie rabochei sily na promyshlennykh predpriyatiyakh*, Moscow, 1965.
7   Breslauer, George W., *Khrushchev and Brezhnev as Leaders: Building Authority in Soviet Politics*, George Allen & Unwin, London, 1982.
8   Brown, J.F., *The New Eastern Europe: The Khrushchev Era*, Praeger, New York, 1966.
9   Brzezinski, Z.B., *The Soviet Bloc: Unity and Conflict*, Harvard University Press, Cambridge, MA, 1967.
10 Brus, Wlodzimierz, *Socialist Ownership and Political Systems*, Routledge & Kegan Paul, London, 1975.
11 Bunce, Valerie, *Do New Leaders Make a Difference? Executive Succession and Public Policy under Capitalism and Socialism*, Princeton University Press, Princeton, NJ, 1981.
12 Burlatsky, Fedor, 'Khrushchev: Shtrikhi k politicheskomy portrety', *Literaturnaya gazeta*, 24 Feb. 1988.
13 Chotiner, Barbara Ann, *Khrushchev's Party Reforms. Coalition Building and Institutional Innovation*, Greenwood Press, Westport, CT, 1984.
14 Clissold, Stephen (ed.), *Soviet Relations with Latin America 1918–1968*, Oxford University Press, Oxford, 1970.
15 Clissold, Stephen (ed.), *Yugoslavia and the Soviet Union 1939–73*, Oxford University Press, Oxford, 1975.
16 Cohen, Stephen F., Rabinowitch A. and Sharlet, Robert (eds), *The Soviet Union since Stalin*, Macmillan, London, 1980.

17   Conquest, Robert, *Power and Policy in the USSR*, Harper, New York, 1961.
18   Crankshaw, Edward, *Khrushchev's Russia*, Penguin, Harmondsworth, 1959.
19   Crankshaw, Edward, *Khrushchev*, Viking Press, New York, 1966.
20   Danilova, E.Z., *Sotsialnye problemy truda zhenshchiny-rabotnitsy*, Moscow, 1968.
21   Davies, R.W., 'The Reappraisal of Industry', *Soviet Studies*, Jan. 1956.
22   Deutscher, Isaac, 'Khrushchev on Stalin', in *Ironies of History*, Oxford University Press, Oxford, 1966.
23   Fainsod, Merle, *How Russia is Ruled*, 2nd edn, Harvard University Press, Cambridge, MA, 1963.
24   Fainsod, Merle, 'Khrushchevism', in Milorad M. Drachkovitch (ed.), *Marxism in the Modern World*, Stanford University Press, Stanford, CA, 1965.
25   Fainsod, Merle, 'Khrushchevism in Retrospect', *Problems of Communism*, no. 1, Jan.–Feb. 1965.
26   Filtzer, Donald, *The Khrushchev Era: De-Stalinization and the Limits of Reform in the USSR, 1953–1964*, Macmillan, London, 1993.
27   Filtzer, Donald, 'The Soviet Wage Reform of 1956–1962', *Soviet Studies* (1), Jan. 1989.
28   Filtzer, Donald, *Soviet Workers and De-Stalinization: The Consolidation of the Modern System of Soviet Production Relations, 1953–1964*, Cambridge University Press, Cambridge, 1992.
29   Frankland, Mark, *Khrushchev*, Stein & Day, New York, 1967.
30   Garthoff, Raymond L., *Soviet Military Policy*, Faber & Faber, London, 1966.
31   Gliksman, Jerzy, 'Recent Trends in Soviet Labor Legislation', *Problems of Communism*, July–Aug. 1956.
32   Gromyko, A.A., *Pamyatnoe*, 2 vols, Izdatelstvo Politicheskoi Literatury, Moscow, 1988.
33   Gromyko, Andrei, *Memories*, trans. by Harold Shukman, Hutchinson, London, 1989.
34   Gruliow, Leo (ed.), *Current Soviet Policies: The Documentary Record of the Nineteenth Communist Party Congress and the Reorganization after Stalin's Death*, Praeger, New York, 1953.
35   Gruliow, Leo (ed.), *Current Soviet Policies II: The Documentary Record of the 20th Communist Party Congress and its Aftermath*, Praeger, New York, 1957.
36   Gruliow, Leo (ed.) *Current Soviet Policies III: The Documentary Record of the Extraordinary 21st Congress of the Communist Party of the Soviet Union*, Columbia University Press, New York, 1960.
37   Gruliow, Leo, and Saikowski, Charlotte (eds), *Current Soviet Policies IV: The Documentary Record of the 22nd Congress of the Communist Party of the Soviet Union*, Columbia University Press, New York, 1962.

38 Gruliow, Leo *et al.* (eds), *Current Soviet Policies V: The Documentary Record of the 23rd Congress of the Communist Party of the Soviet Union*, American Association for the Advancement of Slavic Studies, Columbus, Ohio, 1973.

39 Hahn, W.G., *The Politics of Soviet Agriculture, 1960–1970*, Johns Hopkins University Press, Baltimore, MD, 1972.

40 Hodnett, Grey, 'Succession Contingencies in the Soviet Union', *Problems of Communism*, March–April 1975.

41 Holubenko, M., 'The Soviet Working Class: Discontent and Opposition', *Critique*, no. 4, 1975.

42 Horelick, Arnold, and Rush, Myron, *Strategic Power and Soviet Foreign Policy*, University of Chicago Press, Chicago, IL, 1966.

43 Hosking, Geoffrey, *A History of the Soviet Union*, Fontana Press/Collins, London, 1985.

44 Hough, Jerry, 'A hare-brained scheme in retrospect', *Problems of Communism*, March–April 1976.

45 Hough, Jerry, 'The party apparatchiki', in H. Gordon Skilling and Franklyn Griffiths (eds), *Interest Groups in Soviet Politics*, Princeton University Press, Princeton, NJ, 1971.

46 Hough, Jerry, *Soviet Leadership in Transition*, Brookings Institution, Washington, DC, 1980.

47 Hough, Jerry, *The Soviet Prefects*, Harvard University Press, Cambridge, MA, 1968.

48 Hough, Jerry, and Fainsod, Merle, *How the Soviet Union is Governed*, Harvard University Press, Cambridge, MA, 1979.

49 Hyland, William, and Shryock, Richard Wallace, *The Fall of Khrushchev*, Macmillan, London, 1970.

50 Johnson, Priscilla, *Khrushchev and the Arts*, MIT Press, Cambridge, MA, 1965.

51 Joravsky, David, *The Lysenko Affair*, Harvard University Press, Cambridge, MA, 1970.

52 Kanet, Roger, 'The Rise and Fall of the All-People's State, Recent Changes in the Soviet Theory of the State', *Soviet Studies*, July 1968.

53 Karcz, J.F., *The Economics of Soviet Agriculture*, Indiana University Press, Bloomington, IN, 1979.

54 Katsenelinbogen, Aron, *Soviet Economic Thought and Political Power in the USSR*, Pergamon, London, 1980.

55 Katz, Abraham, *The Politics of Economic Reform in the Soviet Union*, Pall Mall Press, London, 1973.

56 Khrushchev, N.S., *Vospominaniya: Izbrannye otryvki*, Chalidze Press, New York, 1979.

57 Khrushchev, Nikita, *Khrushchev Remembers*, with an introduction, commentary and notes by Edward Crankshaw, trans. by Strobe Talbott, Sphere Books, London, 1971.

58 Khrushchev, Nikita, *Khrushchev Remembers*, vol. 1, trans. and ed. by Strobe Talbott, Little, Brown Boston, 1970.

59   Khrushchev, Nikita, *Khrushchev Remembers: The Last Testament*,
     vol. 2, trans. and ed. by Strobe Talbott, Little, Brown, Boston,
     1974.
60   Khrushchev, Nikita, *Khrushchev Remembers: The Glasnost Tapes*
     with a foreword by Strobe Talbott, trans. and ed. by Jerrold L.
     Schecter and Vyacheslav V. Luchkov, Little, Brown, Boston, 1974.
61   Khrushchev, N.S., *Stroitelstvo kommunizma v SSR u razvitie
     selskogo khozyaistva*, 8 vols, Izdatelstvo Politicheskoi Literatury,
     Moscow, 1962–64.
62   Khrushchev, Sergei, *Khrushchev on Khrushchev: An Inside Account
     of the Man and His Era, by His Son*, Little, Brown, Boston, 1992.
63   Khrushchev, N.S., *The 'Secret' Speech Delivered to the Closed
     Session of the Twentieth Congress of the Communist Party of the
     Soviet Union*, with an introduction by Zhores A. Medvedev and
     Roy A. Medvedev, Spokesman Books, Nottingham, 1976.
64   Kirsch, Leonard, *Soviet Wages: Changes in Structure and
     Administration since 1956*, MIT Press, Cambridge, MA, 1972.
65   Knight, Amy, *Beria: Stalin's First Lieutenant*, Princeton University
     Press, Princeton, NJ, 1993.
66   Laird, Roy D. 'Khrushchev's Administrative Reforms in Agriculture:
     an Appraisal' in J.F. Karcz (ed.), *Soviet and East European
     Agriculture*, University of California Press, Berkeley and Los
     Angeles, CA, 1967.
67   Kolkowicz, Roman, *The Soviet Military and the Communist Party*,
     Princeton University Press, Princeton, NJ, 1967.
68   Laird, Roy D. (ed.), *Soviet Agricultural and Peasant Affairs*,
     University of Kansas Press, Kansas, KS, 1964.
69   Leonhard, Wolfgang, *The Kremlin since Stalin*, Praeger, New York,
     1962.
70   Levi, Arrigo, 'The Evolution of the Soviet System', in Zbigniew
     Brzezinski (ed.), *Dilemmas of Change in Soviet Politics*, Columbia
     University Press, New York, 1969.
71   Levine, Herbert, 'Pressure and Planning in the Soviet Economy', in
     Henry Rosovsky (ed.), *Industrialization in Two Systems: Essays in
     Honor of Alexander Gerschenkron*, Wiley, New York, 1966.
72   Linden, Carl, *Khrushchev and the Soviet Leadership 1957–1964*,
     Johns Hopkins University Press, Baltimore, MD, 1966.
73   McAuley, Mary, *Labour Disputes in Soviet Russia 1957–1965*,
     Clarendon Press, Oxford, 1969.
74   McAuley, Mary, *Politics and the Soviet Union*, Penguin,
     Harmondsworth, 1978.
75   McCauley, Martin, *Khrushchev and the Development of Soviet
     Agriculture: The Virgin Lands Programme 1953–1964*, Macmillan,
     London, 1976.
76   McCauley, Martin, (ed.), *Khrushchev and Khrushchevism*,
     Macmillan, London, 1987.

77   McCauley, Martin, *Nikita Sergeevich Khrushchev*, Cardinal, London, 1991.
78   McCauley, Martin, *The Soviet Union 1917–1991*, Longman, London, 1993.
79   Matthews, Mervyn, *Class and Society in Soviet Russia*, Allen & Unwin, London, 1972.
80   Medvedev, Roy A., *All Stalin's Men*, Oxford University Press, Oxford, 1983.
81   Medvedev, Roy A., *Khrushchev*, Basil Blackwell, Oxford, 1983.
82   Medvedev, Roy A., *Let History Judge*, Oxford University Press, Oxford, 1989.
83   Medvedev, Roy and Medvedev, Zhores, *Khrushchev: The Years in Power*, Oxford University Press, Oxford, 1977.
84   Medvedev, Zhores, *The Rise and Fall of T.D. Lysenko*, Columbia University Press, New York, 1969.
85   Medvedev, Zhores, *Soviet Agriculture*, W.W. Norton, New York, 1987.
86   Micunovic, V., *Moscow Diary*, Doubleday, New York, 1980.
87   Miller, R.F. and Féhér F. (eds), *Khrushchev and the Communist World*, Croom Helm, London, 1984.
88   Nicolaevsky, Boris, *Power and the Soviet Elite*, Praeger, New York, 1965.
89   Nogee Joseph L. and Donaldson, Robert H., *Soviet Foreign Policy since World War II*, Pergamon, New York, 1984.
90   Nove, Alec, *An Economic History of the USSR*, rev. ed., Penguin, Harmondsworth, 1992.
91   Paloczi-Horvath, George, *Khrushchev: The Road to Power*, Secker & Warburg, London, 1960.
92   Pethybridge, Roger, *A Key to Soviet Politics: The Crisis of the 'Anti-Party' Group*, Allen & Unwin, London, 1962.
93   Pinkus, Benjamin, *The Soviet Government and the Jews, 1948–1967*, Cambridge University Press, Cambridge, 1984.
94   Ploss, Sidney, *Conflict and Decision Making in Soviet Russia: A Case Study of Agricultural Policy, 1953–1963*, Princeton University Press, Princeton, NJ, 1965.
95   Rigby, T.H., *Communist Party Membership in the USSR, 1917–1967*, Princeton University Press, Princeton, N.J., 1968.
96   Rigby, T.H., Brown, Archie and Reddaway, Peter (eds) *Authority, Power and Policy in the USSR*, St Martin's Press, New York, 1980.
97   Ro'i, Yaacov, *The Struggle for Soviet-Jewish Emigration*, Cambridge University Press, Cambridge, 1989.
98   Rothberg, Abraham, *The Heirs of Stalin*, Cornell University Press, Ithaca, NY, 1972.
99   Rush, Myron, *Political Succession in the Soviet Union*, 2nd edn, Columbia University Press, New York, 1968.

100   Rush, Myron, *The Rise of Khrushchev*, Public Affairs Press, Washington, DC, 1958.

101   Schapiro, Leonard, *The Communist Party of the Soviet Union*, Methuen, London 1963.

102   Schapiro, Leonard (ed.), *The USSR and the Future: An Analysis of the New Program of the CPSU*, Praeger, New York, 1963.

103   Schwartz, Harry, *The Soviet Economy since Stalin*, Lippincott, Philadelphia, PA, 1965.

104   Service, Robert, J., 'The Road to the Twentieth Party Congress: An Analysis of the Events Surrounding the Central Committee Plenum of July 1953', *Soviet Studies*, xxxiii, (2), 1981.

105   Simon, Gerhard, *Nationalismus und Nationitätenpolitik in der Sowjetunion: Von der totalitären Diktatur zur nachstalinischen Gesellschaft*, Nomos Verlagsgesellschaft, Baden Baden, 1986.

106   Simon, Gerhard, *Nationalism and Policy toward the Nationalities in the Soviet Union: From Totalitarian Dictatorship to Post-Stalinist Society*, Westview Press, Boulder, CO, 1991.

107   Slusser, Robert M., *The Berlin Crisis of 1961*, Johns Hopkins University Press, Baltimore, MD, 1973.

108   Spechler, Dina, 'Permitted Dissent in the Decade after Stalin', in Paul Cocks, Robert Daniels and Nancy Heer (eds), *The Dynamics of Soviet Politics*, Harvard University Press, Cambridge, MA, 1976.

109   Strauss, Erich, *Soviet Agriculture in Perspective*, Allen & Unwin, London, 1969.

110   Swayze, Harold, *Political Control of Literature in the USSR, 1946–1959*, Harvard University Press, Cambridge, MA, 1962.

111   Tatu, Michel, *Power in the Kremlin: From Khrushchev's Decline to Collective Leadership*, Viking Press, New York, 1969.

112   Taubman, William, *Governing Soviet Cities*, Praeger, New York, 1973.

113   Tompson, William J., *Khrushchev: A Political Life*, Macmillan, London, 1995.

114   Ulam, Adam, *Expansion and Coexistence*, 2nd edn, Praeger, New York, 1974.

115   Ulam, Adam B., *A History of Soviet Russia*, Praeger, New York, 1976.

116   Ungar, Aryeh, *The Totalitarian Party*, Cambridge University Press, Cambridge, 1974.

117   Van den Berg, G.P., *Organisation und Arbeitsweise der sowjetischen Regierung*, Nomos Verlagsgesellschaft, Baden Baden, 1984.

118   Wädekin, Karl-Eugen, *The Private Sector in Soviet Agriculture*, University of California Press, Berkeley and Los Angeles, CA, 1973.

119   Whitefield, Stephen, *Industrial Power and the Soviet State*, Clarendon Press, Oxford, 1993.

120   Wolfe, Bertram D., *Khrushchev and Stalin's Ghost*, Praeger, New York, 1957.

121 *XXII-y sezd KPSS: Stenografichesky otchet Politicheskoe Izdatelstvo*, Moscow, vol. 2, 1961.

122 Yevtushenko, Y., *A Precocious Autobiography*, Faber & Faber, London 1963.

INDEX